C. Ernst

A HANDBOOK OF
AIDS
FOR TEACHING
JUNIOR—SENIOR
HIGH SCHOOL
MATHEMATICS

STEPHEN KRULIK

Temple University, Philadelphia

1971   W. B. SAUNDERS COMPANY • PHILADELPHIA • LONDON • TORONTO

W. B. Saunders Company: West Washington Square
Philadelphia, Pa. 19105

12 Dyott Street
London, WC1A   1DB

1835 Yonge Street
Toronto 7, Ontario

A Handbook of Aids for Teaching Junior and Senior High School Mathematics   SBN   0-7216-5540-8

Print No.:   9   8   7   6   5   4   3   2   1

INTRODUCTION

Since the start of the so-called "Revolution in Mathematics Education" that began in the late 1950s, there has been a great deal of controversy as to just what should comprise modern mathematics education. Should it consist in new ideas, new content, a new approach to teaching methods, or a combination of all three of these? Regardless of how this problem is finally resolved, teachers agree that there will be a change within the traditional secondary school mathematics classroom. Educators generally agree that the key factor in any kind of learning experience is the method or process through which actual learning takes place.

Today, pupils are being forced to learn more and more mathematics in the same amount of time, and are expected to understand what they learn much more thoroughly; the teacher is faced with this problem. Mathematics must be taught for much more than the mere achievement of computational skills. Today, many educators feel that for optimum results, mathematics should be taught from a discovery approach, an approach that encourages the learner to manipulate devices, to play mathematical games, to gather data, and to form his own conclusions. In other words, the pupil is supposed to become involved in mathematics learning as an active participant, not as a "tell-me-about-it" passive listener. As a result of this approach, the mathematics teacher must develop, construct, and use aids as often as possible, aids that do not depend solely upon the ability to read for their use, as does the textbook.

In the elementary school grades, teacher training institutions have emphasized this laboratory approach for some time. Multi-sensory aids for mathematics teaching at this level is the norm, rather than the unusual. On the secondary school level, however, this approach for many teachers is new. Some secondary school mathematics teachers have never used an aid other than their textbook, a filmstrip, or a film. Consequently, there is not as much organized source material for the junior and senior high school teacher of mathematics available as he would like. This manual is an attempt to provide some source material.

Let me stress that this manual is by no means a complete sourcebook. Its very nature prohibits it from being one. Every teacher in every school has some favorite aid or gadget that someone has developed and used successfully in teaching mathematics. Many textbooks on mathematics methodology offer one or two sample aids for the new teacher to use. Imaginative teachers have generally created new aids as their situations called for them.

This book is an attempt to gather and organize a few of the many aids available. Each aid presented has been used by teachers of mathematics. You may recognize some of the aids; others will be new to you. You will probably think of many functions for a particular aid in addition to those suggested. Feel free to use these aids in any way you find suitable. The success of any aid depends on you, the teacher in the classroom. You should be limited only by the confines of your own imagination.

As you read through this book, you will notice some empty pages. These are not printer's errors; they are there intentionally. This book is a personal kind of manual. Give it that personal touch. Use these blank pages to make notes. Was the aid easy to make? Did you spot any tricks in making it? At what point in your classwork did you use the aid? How did your students respond to it? What mathematical ideas were developed in its use? Would you use it again? With what class? Would you modify it next time? Would you ignore it next time?

The answers to these and other questions that arise in using this handbook and any comments you may wish to make are the things that will enhance its value as a personal source of material for your own mathematics teaching.

You have in your hand the ideas of many creative teachers. Like all ideas, they are only valuable when they are used. Good luck!

CONTENTS

SECTION FOUR   TRIGONOMETRY

SECTION FIVE   MISCELLANEOUS

SECTION ONE

PRE-ALGEBRA

NAPIER BONES — MECHANICAL MULTIPLICATION

It is often very difficult to encourage secondary school mathematics students to practice the basic multiplication processes that need strengthening. Unfortunately, they consider this "babyish" and beneath them, especially at the junior high school level. It is possible to work with these fundamental skills by making and using the Napier rods, or Napier bones as they are often called. The pupils are quite interested in the concept of these rods as an early introduction to the computer age.

MAKING THE BONES

Use either wooden tongue depressors, or strips of posterboard. Each student should have his own set to work with. A set requires eleven vertical strips, each about ten inches long and one inch wide. Each strip is divided into ten congruent squares. The squares are then divided along a diagonal. The multiplication facts for each of the integers from one to nine are placed on the respective rods. One rod, with no diagonal divisions, is the INDEX rod. This rod contains the digits from one to nine.

USING THE BONES

Suppose we wish to multiply 432 by 4. Place the rods for 4, 3, and 2 next to each other. Align the INDEX rod at the left. The products are then read along the diagonal by adding the numbers as shown in figure 2.

If we wish to extend the use of these rods to multiplication by a two digit multiplier, we can do so. Suppose we wish to multiply 432 by 53. We place the rods for 4, 3, and 2 next to each other with our INDEX rod at the left. After reading the result of 432 multiplied by 3, we read the answer for 432 multiplied by 5. This second product is then *multiplied by 10* and written underneath. Thus, 432 × 3 = 1,296; 432 × 5 = 2,160. Multiply this answer by ten and we obtain 21,600. Adding, we find that 432 × 53 = 22,896.

INDEX	1	2	3	4	5	6	7	8	9	0
1	0/1	0/2	0/3	0/4	0/5	0/6	0/7	0/8	0/9	0/0
2	0/2	0/4	0/6	0/8	1/0	1/2	1/4	1/6	1/8	0/0
3	0/3	0/6	0/9	1/2	1/5	1/8	2/1	2/4	2/7	0/0
4	0/4	0/8	1/2	1/6	2/0	2/4	2/8	3/2	3/6	0/0
5	0/5	1/0	1/5	2/0	2/5	3/0	3/5	4/0	4/5	0/0
6	0/6	1/2	1/8	2/4	3/0	3/6	4/2	4/8	5/4	0/0
7	0/7	1/4	2/1	2/8	3/5	4/2	4/9	5/6	6/3	0/0
8	0/8	1/6	2/4	3/2	4/0	4/8	5/6	6/4	7/2	0/0
9	0/9	1/8	2/7	3/6	4/5	5/4	6/3	7/2	8/1	0/0

Figure 1. Napier bones.

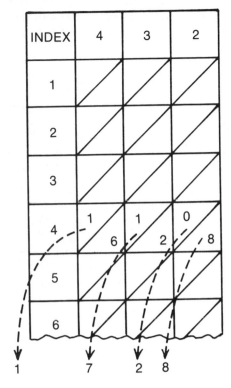

Figure 2. 432 X 4.

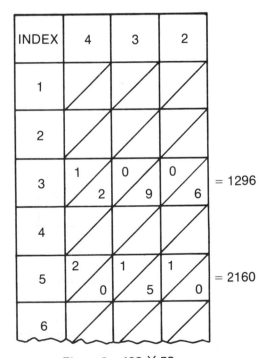

Figure 3. 432 X 53.

-It is interesting to note that the Napier bones can be made in number bases other than ten. Here for example, are the bones for base four. Notice that only four bones are needed:

INDEX	1	2	3	0
1	0 / 1	0 / 2	0 / 3	0 / 0
2	0 / 2	1 / 0	1 / 2	0 / 0
3	0 / 3	1 / 2	2 / 1	0 / 0

Figure 4. Napier bones – base 4.

The procedure for using the bones in bases other than ten is the same. Thus, if we wish to multiply 23(base 4) by 3, we select the rods for 2 and 3 from our base four set, and place the INDEX rod alongside:

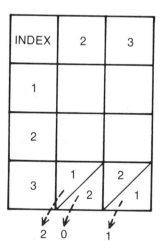

Figure 5. Multiplying – base 4.

Notice that the addition of 2 + 2 in base four leads to a 10(base 4) result. This gives the answer, 201(base 4).

This device provides an excellent review for work in number bases, other than base ten.

NUMBER GRIDS

Many teachers look for ideas in everyday media that can be adapted to their mathematics classes. Several magazines have carried letter grids, with the names of the fifty states hidden in them. This idea is easily extended to a mathematics grid that can be used to stimulate thought and enjoyment on the part of the students. At the same time, it provides a review drill in the fundamental operations of arithmetic. These grids can be challenging at any level, if carefully designed.

MAKING THE GRID

The grid is simply an array of numbers. These should be carefully thought out, so as to provide many possible combinations for the students to recognize. A simple grid for the fundamental operations of arithmetic might be one similar to the following:

USING THE GRID

Each student should be given a copy of the grid which has previously been duplicated. The student is to discover any true mathematical statement within the grid, by putting in the operational symbols, and the equality symbol. Parentheses may also be used. Numbers may be used more than once. Statements can be made horizontally, vertically and diagonally. Students using the grid will often notice involved mathematical concepts such as inverse operations ($7 \times 3 = 21$ or $7 = 21 \div 3$), commutative, associative, distributive laws, and so forth.

Some possible solutions on the given grid might include:

9	6	3	81	42	7	6	19	23
45	2	3	27	8	6	8	25	8
5	7	18	3	5	1	14	7	15
21	4	4	9	6	14	3	11	5
58	7	4	28	2	15	2	9	75
3	18	7	2	5	10	8	3	12
36	9	49	14	2	28	42	7	63
7	6	7	36	9	4	50	3	11
32	54	6	9	8	3	6	5	12

Figure 6.

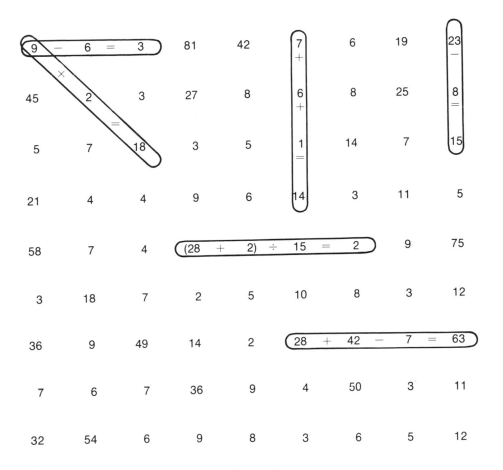

Figure 7.

FRACTION CUBES

Many students at the junior high school level are very weak when it comes to performing the fundamental operations on fractions. This is especially true for the operation of addition of fractions with different denominators. Unfortunately, students at this level often refuse to work at this necessary review task. As a result, the teacher is faced with the problem of developing games that will enable the pupils to enjoy participating in this review, without realizing that it is a review.

MAKING THE CUBES

From a lumber yard, it is possible to obtain pieces of wood one inch wide, one inch thick, and twelve to twenty-four inches long. These are easily cut into blocks, one inch by one inch by one inch. These blocks are then finished with sandpaper, and, if desired, painted in bright colors. On each face of the cube, place a fraction. This may be in simplest form (such as 3/4) or it may be in some other equivalent form (as 9/12). Use as many fractions with different denominators from two to twelve as possible.

USING THE CUBES

The game may be played by groups of two to four students. Each player in turn rolls the two cubes. The players in his group must add the two fractions that land face up on these cubes. The first student to get the correct answer receives one point. To make the game a little more challenging, a third cube can be added. The pupils must now add three fractions quickly. The game ends with either a time limit, or when a pre-determined point total is reached by one student in the group.

Another variation on this game is to ask the students to find the *difference* between the larger and smaller of the two fractions shown. This requires a bit more effort, since the pupils must determine which fraction has the larger value before subtracting.

FRACTION "WAR" — CARD GAME

Card games are probably the easiest of all aids for a teacher to make. The only physical materials required are a series of small cards made of posterboard, oaktag, or some similar material, and a felt-tipped marking pen. The variety of games possible is virtually endless.

On the other hand, however, the very nature of card games usually limits the number of students who can participate in a particular game at any one time. As a result, the teacher must either make several sets of the same deck of cards for a particular game, or else have a rotating series of card games going on at the same time. In this latter case, the group of students will move from game to game after a fifteen to twenty minute time period (or any other pre-determined time limit).

Notice, too, that it is not always necessary to have every student in the class playing card games at the same time. Some students could be doing classwork, homework, or working with another aid. The teacher would be spared the task of making classroom sets of each aid if he planned for diversity of activities; the students would probably be much happier, too.

Noise tolerance, too, becomes a factor. Students enjoy the competitive element; they often get into heated discussions and arguments over the game. The teacher must be prepared for a great deal of noise in the classroom. However, this is good noise; it is constructive noise. Furthermore, if diverse activities are carefully planned for, it is possible to keep the number of students involved in games to a minimum. This will keep the noise factor down.

Fraction War is a card game that can be used successfully to review and strengthen work in fractions, especially in comparing their size. It involves finding a common denominator, and changing the given fractions to equivalent fractions. The game can be played by two, three, or four students at one time.

MAKING THE DECK

1. The deck consists of sixty-six cards, each approximately three inches by two and one-half inches in size. These cards can easily be made by cutting ordinary three inch by five inch file cards in half.

2. On each card, write one of the following common fractions, being careful *not* to reduce to lowest terms:

$$\frac{1}{2}, \frac{1}{3}, \frac{2}{3}, \frac{1}{4}, \frac{2}{4}, \frac{3}{4}, \frac{1}{5}, \frac{2}{5}, \frac{3}{5}, \frac{4}{5}, \frac{1}{6}, \frac{2}{6}, \frac{3}{6}, \frac{4}{6},$$

$$\frac{5}{6}, \frac{1}{7}, \frac{2}{7}, \frac{3}{7}, \frac{4}{7}, \frac{5}{7}, \frac{6}{7}, \frac{1}{8}, \frac{2}{8}, \frac{3}{8}, \frac{4}{8}, \frac{5}{8}, \frac{6}{8}, \frac{7}{8},$$

$$\frac{1}{9}, \frac{2}{9}, \frac{3}{9}, \frac{4}{9}, \frac{5}{9}, \frac{6}{9}, \frac{7}{9}, \frac{8}{9}, \frac{1}{10}, \frac{2}{10}, \frac{3}{10}, \frac{4}{10}, \frac{5}{10}, \frac{6}{10},$$

$$\frac{7}{10}, \frac{8}{10}, \frac{9}{10}, \frac{1}{11}, \frac{2}{11}, \frac{3}{11}, \frac{4}{11}, \frac{5}{11}, \frac{6}{11}, \frac{7}{11}, \frac{8}{11}, \frac{9}{11}, \frac{10}{11}, \frac{1}{12},$$

$$\frac{2}{12}, \frac{3}{12}, \frac{4}{12}, \frac{5}{12}, \frac{6}{12}, \frac{7}{12}, \frac{8}{12}, \frac{9}{12}, \frac{10}{12}, \frac{11}{12}$$

3. Each player also has some scrap paper and a pencil with which to make his computations.

PLAYING THE GAME

1. The deck is shuffled and dealt face down to the players in turn, until all the cards have been distributed.

2. Each player keeps his cards face down in front of him.

3. Each player turns his top card face up. The players must then decide which card shows the fraction having the greatest value. The scrap paper is used to do this.

4. The player whose card has the fraction with the highest value takes all the cards that were turned up and places them face down at the bottom of his pack of cards.

5. In the event of a tie (i.e., two equivalent fractions are turned up such as 2/3 or 8/12, for example) a "war" is declared. Each of the players involved in the war places the next three cards from his pack face down. He turns over the fourth card. The person with the fraction of highest value now showing takes all the cards involved in the "war."

6. Play continues in a similar manner until one player has lost all his cards, or until time is called. In this latter case, the winner is the player with the most cards at the end of the time period.

FRACTION "GO FISH" ✓
— CARD GAME

Most pupils enjoy the competitive nature of card games. They participate widely, and compete intensely. They get deeply involved, and often generate heated discussions, which, in themselves, provide an excellent vehicle for learning. (This card game is another adaptation of a traditional card game to help encourage students to review work with fractions at the junior high school level.) *Elem. or*

MAKING THE DECK

1. The deck consists of any number of cards desired. Each is approximately three inches by two and one-half inches in size. These can be made by cutting ordinary three inch by five inch file cards in half.

2. On each card, write one common fraction such as 1/2, 1/4, 3/4, 6/8, 5/10, 1/3, 4/12. Be careful not to reduce any of the fractions to lowest terms. Have as many pairs of equivalent fractions in the deck as possible.

3. Be certain that every fraction has at least one equivalent form somewhere in the deck.

4. Provide each student with scrap paper and a pencil for computation.

USING THE DECK

1. Each pupil playing the game should receive either five or seven cards, depending upon the number of players. Limit the number of participants to four. The balance of the deck is placed face down, in the center of the playing table.

2. All players begin by discarding any pairs of equivalent fractions they may have in their hand. These are placed face up in the center of the table.

3. The first player (usually the dealer) asks any other specific player if he has a particular card to enable him to make a pair. For example, player number one might have a card with 15/20 on it. He might ask player number three,

"Do you have a card with 3/4 on it?" If player number three has a card with any equivalent form of 3/4 on it, he must give it to player who asked for it. This gives player number one a pair, which he can discard. He then may continue in a similar manner until he asks for a card that a player does not have.

4. When the player asked does not have a requested card, the player asking must "go fish" from the pack in the center, picking the top card. Play then passes to the player to the right.

5. The winner of the game is the first to discard all the cards in his hand, by throwing out pairs of equivalent fractions. If no one succeeds in discarding all his cards, the winner is the player with the fewest cards remaining when the pack in the center is gone.

6. A more difficult variation of this game is to have pupils discard only pairs of cards whose sum is one. Thus, a player might discard a card having 15/20 on it, if he could find a card with 1/4 on it.

MAGIC SQUARES

Students on the secondary school level sometimes need practice in addition. It is difficult to have these children add long columns of figures; they resent this "baby" work and refuse to do it. A good approach to addition is to use a series of magic squares. These arrays of numbers will give the students practice without their being aware of what it is they are doing.

Traditionally, the magic square is a set of integers beginning with one, arranged in a square array, so that the sum of any horizontal row, vertical column, or diagonal is always the same. Today, we often use magic squares with fractions, negative integers, or even decimal fractions.

MAKING THE SQUARES

The easiest square to start with is the three by three magic square. In this square, each row, column, and diagonal add up to fifteen. This could be duplicated and distributed to the pupils.

2	7	6
9	5	1
4	3	8

Figure 8. The basic 3 X 3 magic square.

After the pupils understand what it is that the teacher wants, they can be given a blank three by three array, and asked to fill it in with the positive integers from four to twelve. In this case, the sum of the integers in any row, column or diagonal is twenty-four:

7	12	5
6	8	10
11	4	9

Figure 9.

Another possible three by three square utilizes the integers from seven to fifteen:

14	7	12
9	11	13
10	15	8

Figure 10.

Each pupil should always be required to verify that his array is actually a magic square.

If the class is enjoying this activity, and is a reasonably apt group, they can work on a four by four magic square using the positive integers from one to sixteen. This will usually take some time, and will require some help by the teacher. Be very careful with this one; the students will come up with many variations.

14	11	5	4
7	2	16	9
12	13	3	6
1	8	10	15

Figure 11. A 4 X 4 magic square.

It is possible to make use of the magic square approach with fractions. Magic squares can be designed with missing components, but with one row, column, or diagonal completed. This will involve addition and/or subtraction of the fractions, often a much needed practice.

1/2	1/12	
7/12	5/12	
2/12		

Figure 12. A 3 X 3 fraction magic square.

SIEVE OF ERATOSTHENES

One of the many ideas that mathematicians have pursued down throughout the ages, has been the development of a prime-producing expression. Since many arithmeticians regard prime numbers as the building blocks from which all other integers are made via multiplication, it is only natural that these integers should be studied carefully through the ages. Eratosthenes lived about 230 B.C. His "sieve" is a mechanical method for locating all prime integers less than a given integer, n, and can also be used to find pairs of so-called "twin primes." These are prime numbers that differ by two, such as 17 and 19, or 11 and 13.

MAKING THE SIEVE

On a duplicating master, type or print the integers from one to n. For organizational purposes, n = 100 is a large enough array to work with. By putting the numbers in a columnar array as shown, the material is well organized for use by the students. In a junior high school class, each student should have his own sieve to work with. While the teacher can reproduce a copy on the chalkboard, a larger, demonstration size sieve can be made by pasting a sheet of paper over a piece of pegboard, and writing the numbers in a similar array. Place the numbers over the holes, to make punching them out easy to do.

SIEVE OF ERATOSTHENES

	2	3	4	5	6	7	8	9	10
11	12	13	14	15	16	17	18	19	20
21	22	23	24	25	26	27	28	29	30
31	32	33	34	35	36	37	38	39	40
41	42	43	44	45	46	47	48	49	50
51	52	53	54	55	56	57	58	59	60
61	62	63	64	65	66	67	68	69	70
71	72	73	74	75	76	77	78	79	80
81	82	83	84	85	86	87	88	89	90
91	92	93	94	95	96	97	98	99	100

USING THE SIEVE

1. The students begin by circling the first prime number on their sieve, the number two. They then cross out every succeeding multiple of two (four, six, eight, etc.).

2. The next prime number on the sieve is three. The students circle it. Now, they go through the sieve crossing out all the multiples of three not already crossed out (three, six, nine, etc.).

3. The next prime number left in our sieve is five. The pupils put a circle around it. Now, they cross out all multiples of five not as yet crossed out (five, ten, fifteen, etc.).

4. We do the same thing for seven (circle it; it is a prime) and cross out all the multiples of seven. The numbers remaining in the sieve are all prime numbers less than one hundred.

5. The seven pairs of twin primes will be readily visible among the circled numbers left in the sieve. These twin primes are: 5 and 7; 11 and 13; 17 and 19; 29 and 31; 41 and 43; 59 and 61; 71 and 73.

CROSS NUMBER PUZZLES

Teachers often look for something constructive that students can do when they finish some work earlier than the rest of the class. Many teachers find it advantageous to keep a box of cross number puzzles in a folder in the back of the room. Students are encouraged to go to the back and take a puzzle from the folder when they have time. The puzzles do take a great deal of time to develop, but can be duplicated in class sets of fifty or so, and re-used from semester to semester. They should not be too long or too difficult for the students to complete in a reasonable length of time. They do serve as an excellent vehicle for a painless review.

MAKING THE PUZZLES

The puzzles can be made with only a single operation. For example, an addition puzzle might be this one:

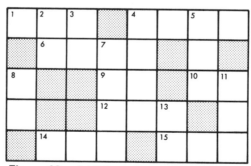

Figure 13. Addition cross number puzzle.

ACROSS
1. 28 + 87 + 133 + 42 + 142
4. 1,327 + 1,327
6. 587 + 932 + 857 + 265
8. 4 + 2
9. 12 + 9 + 7
10. 18 + 12 + 7
12. 84 + 96 + 252 + 181 + 128
14. 126 + 42 + 24 + 18 + 20 + 12 + 10
15. 123 + 98 + 201 + 36

DOWN
2. 18 + 14
3. 9 + 7 + 5 + 3 + 2
4. 1024 + 1024 + 136
5. 47 + 83 + 97 + 184 + 67 + 45
7. 2,136 + 1,068 + 534 + 267 + 267
8. 17 + 32 + 10 + 9
11. 252 + 183 + 197 + 116
13. 6 + 4 + 4

On the other hand, a more general review of the basic operations might involve a more extensive puzzle:

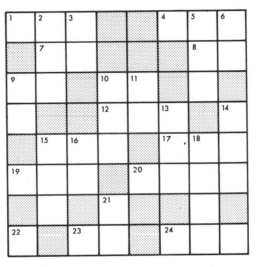

Figure 14. Cross number puzzle.

ACROSS

1. 47×6
4. $(90 \times 6) + 74$
7. $252 \div 4$
8. 11×2
9. 12×7
10. 4^3
12. $(79 \times 9) + 20$
15. 2^8
17. 229×2
19. $3017 \div 7$
20. $(84 \times 19) - 270$
22. A prime between 5 and 11
23. $(7 \times 4) + 3$
24. $(43 \times 12) + (163 \times 2)$

DOWN

2. $3456 \div 4$
3. $2^4 + 7$
5. 2^7
6. $7 \times 3 \times 2$
9. 3^4
10. 26^2
11. A prime between 41 and 47
13. 13×11
14. $3^3 \times 3^2 \times 2$
15. 59×4
16. 17×3
18. $(3^4 \times 4^3) + 20$
21. 9^2

Cross number puzzles can also be developed expressing the numbers in bases other than ten. This will give pupils facility in converting to number bases, and provides an excellent review of this topic.

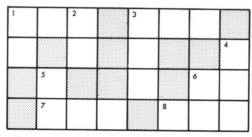

Figure 15.   Cross number puzzle—base 4.

ACROSS

1. Write 18 in base 4
3. Write 32 in base 4
6. Write 13 in base 4
7. Write 42 in base 4
8. Write 25 in base 4

DOWN

1. Write 7 in base 4
2. Write 10 in base 4
3. Write 45 in base 4
4. Write 53 in base 4
5. Write 6 in base 4
6. Write 14 in base 4

NUMBER BASE WAR
— CARD GAME

Once students have done work on numbers in bases other than ten, teachers rarely have the time or the means to review this material, other than by adding numbers in these bases, or by changing back and forth from base ten to or from base b. This card game enables the teacher to review this process of changing from one base to another under a competitive game situation, one in which children will gladly participate.

MAKING THE DECK

1. The deck consists of fifty cards, each approximately three inches by two and one-half inches in size.

2. On each card, place a number from one to ten in some base other than ten. Indicate the base selected. The most commonly used bases are base two, base five, base six, base eight, and possibly base twelve. The cards might look something like this:

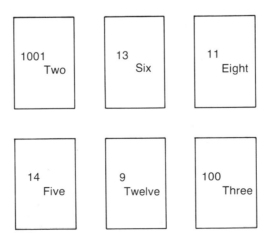

Figure 18. Some cards for number base war. (All have the value nine.)

USING THE DECK

Play is similar to the game of "War" described in Aid Four on page 11. The players try to determine which card turned over has the higher value. Thus, 1001 in base two would beat 12 in base six. The player with the most cards at the end of the prescribed time period is the winner.

MIND READING CARDS
—BASE TWO

Whenever students work with number bases other than base ten, a discussion arises, sooner or later, involving a study of base two. This set of cards will intrigue the pupils, and is guaranteed to arouse their interest in trying to discover why they work.

MAKING THE CARDS

The teacher can prepare a ditto master of each of the following sets of numbers. Each child can then have his own set. The cards can also be prepared by having the pupils copy each set onto three inch by five inch file cards.

Card I										
1	3	5	7	9	11	13	15	17	19	21
23	25	27	29	31	33	35	37	39	41	43
45	47	49	51	53	55	57	59	61	63	

Card II										
2	3	6	7	10	11	14	15	18	19	22
23	26	27	30	31	34	35	38	39	42	43
46	47	50	51	54	55	58	59	62	63	

Card III										
4	5	6	7	12	13	14	15	20	21	22
23	28	29	30	31	36	37	38	39	44	45
46	47	52	53	54	55	60	61	62	63	

Card IV										
8	9	10	11	12	13	14	15	24	25	26
27	28	29	30	31	40	41	42	43	44	45
46	47	56	57	58	59	60	61	62	63	

Card V										
16	17	18	19	20	21	22	23	24	25	26
27	28	29	30	31	48	49	50	51	52	53
54	55	56	57	58	59	60	61	62	63	

Card VI										
32	33	34	35	36	37	38	39	40	41	42
43	44	45	46	47	48	49	50	51	52	53
54	55	56	57	58	59	60	61	62	63	

USING THE CARDS

1. Ask the student to choose any number from one to sixty-three and tell it to a neighbor, but not to the teacher. Now, show him the six mind-reading cards, one at a time. Ask him to point out those cards on which his number appears. After he has done this, you can tell him his number by simply adding up the first number that appears on each card he has selected.

2. After several trials, the students should become interested in why the trick cards work. Let's look at some of these numbers when they are expressed in base two:

Decimal	32	16	8	4	2	1
1						1
2					1	0
3					1	1
4				1	0	0
5				1	0	1
6				1	1	0
7				1	1	1
8			1	0	0	0
9			1	0	0	1
10			1	0	1	0
11			1	0	1	1
12			1	1	0	0
13			1	1	0	1
14			1	1	1	0
15			1	1	1	1
16		1	0	0	0	0

Figure 19. Numbers in base 2.

Notice that all the numbers on Card I (the odd numbers) have a 1 in the units column; all other columns are completely disregarded. All the numbers on Card II have a 1 in the two column; all those on Card III have a 1 in the four column; and so on. Thus one can use the cards to find the number, by adding the headings of the columns in which the 1's appear. The cards form a mini-computer in base two.

SECTION TWO

ALGEBRA

ADDITION SLIDE RULE
—INTEGERS

The prestige that goes with using a slide rule type of aid is something that often encourages students to work. When we introduce the addition of directed numbers, each child can construct his own cardboard slide rule, and then use it to "discover" how to add these numbers without the aid of the mechanical device. This procedure is better than having the teacher give the pupils the "rules" for addition of integers.

MAKING THE SLIDE RULE

Each student should cut two strips of oaktag, posterboard, or cardboard. Each strip should be about eight inches long by one-half inch wide. Mark both strips with a series of congruent, small squares; each should be about one-half inch by one-half inch. Place the numbers from the number line in consecutive squares on each strip. Place zero near the center of each strip. Label one strip the U-scale (upper scale); label the other strip the D-scale (lower scale).

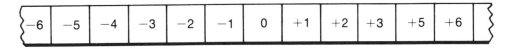

Figure 20.

USING THE SLIDE RULE

Place the strips together with the U-scale on top of the D-scale. Suppose we wish to use our slide rule to add (+4) and (-3). Place the zero on the U-scale directly over the (+4) on the D-scale. Locate the (-3) on the U-scale. Read the result, (+1), on the D-scale, directly beneath the (-3).

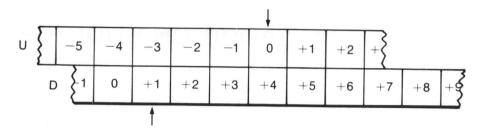

Figure 21. Using the slide rule.

In general, to find the result of a + b using the slide rule, place the zero on the U-scale directly over the a on the D-scale. Locate b on the U-scale. The result can then be read on the D-scale, directly beneath b.

NOMOGRAPH

It is usually desirable for students to "discover" for themselves as much mathematics as possible without being told the so-called rules. In the children's first experiences with positive and negative integers, the nomograph (or nomogram as it is sometimes called) is an excellent device to use in helping the pupils discover the method for addition and subtraction of signed numbers. After several repeated uses of this device, students should be able to formulate a method for addition and subtraction of the integers without using the nomograph.

MAKING THE NOMOGRAPH

Distribute a sheet of graph paper to each pupil. On the graph paper, have the students draw three parallel lines as shown. The Q-scale should be midway between the P-scale and the R-scale. The units on the Q-scale are one-half those on the P and R scales. These are identical. Be certain that the students label these units carefully.

A quicker method for making the nomograph is for the teacher to prepare it in advance on a ditto master, and have one copy for each child. This is not as effective a method, however, since the children profit from actually making the nomograph themselves.

USING THE NOMOGRAPH

To find the sum of two integers, (+3) and (−7) for example, locate (+3) on the P-scale, and (−7) on the R-scale. Connect these two points with either a ruler or actually draw a line. Their sum, (−4), can then be read where the ruler or line crosses the Q-scale.

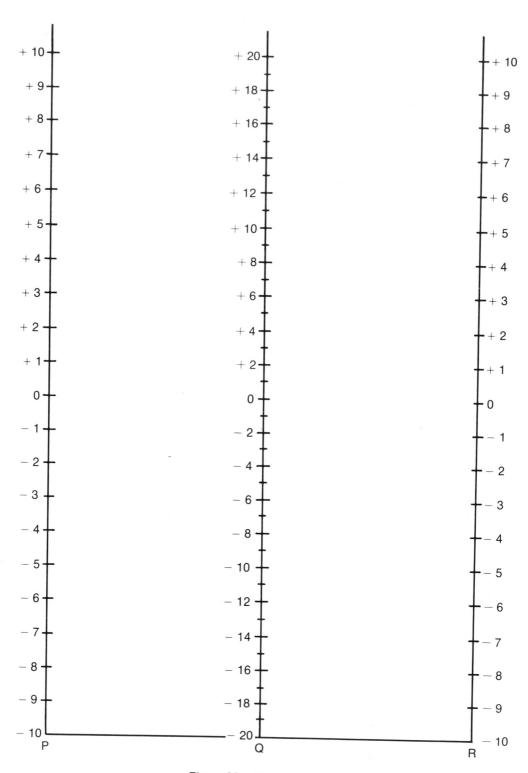

Figure 22. Nomograph.

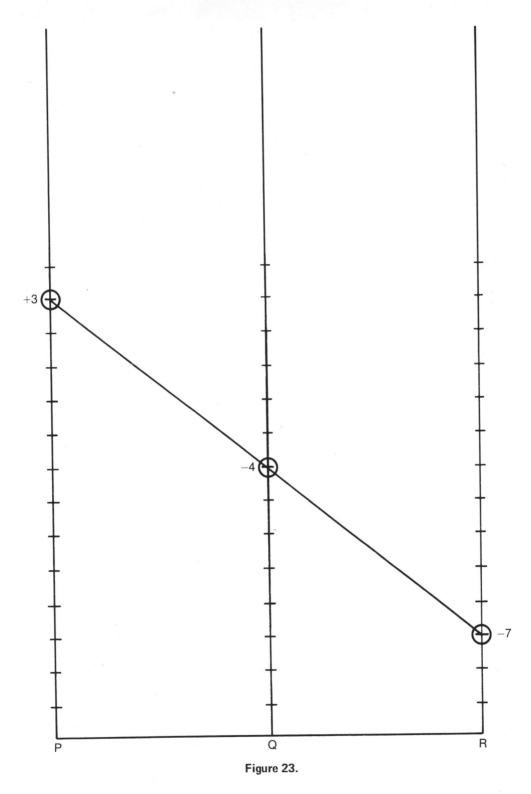

Figure 23.

In general, to add any two integers such as p and r, we locate p on the P-scale and r on the R-scale. If we join points p and r, the line segment pr will cross the Q-scale at a point whose coordinate represents their sum, p + r.

Since we know that p - r = q if and only if p = q + r, we can use this same device for introducing the subtraction of integers. Suppose we wish to find the value of (+6) - (-2). Locate (+6) on our Q-scale, and (-2) on our P-scale. Connect these points and extend the line segment until it cuts the R-scale. Read the difference, (+8), on the R-scale. In general, to find a difference, q - p, locate q on the Q-scale and p on the P-scale. Connect these points, extend the line segment, and read the answer on the R-scale.

A little practice with the nomograph will enable students to make rapid and accurate calculations.

This same device can easily be adapted for addition in number bases other than ten. For example, let us look at a nomograph constructed in base four:

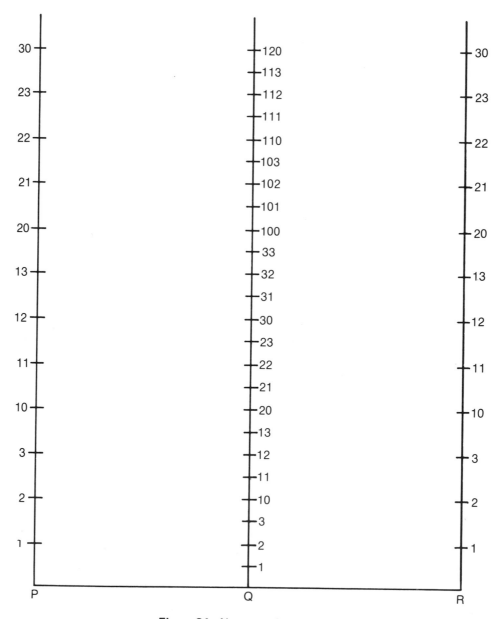

Figure 24. Nomograph — base 4.

Again, the units on the Q-scale are one-half those on the P and R scales. Suppose we wish to use this nomograph to add 22(base 4) and 11(base 4). Locate 22(base 4) on the P-scale and 11(base 4) on the R-scale. Connect these two points. Read the result, 33(base 4) where the line segment crosses the Q-scale.

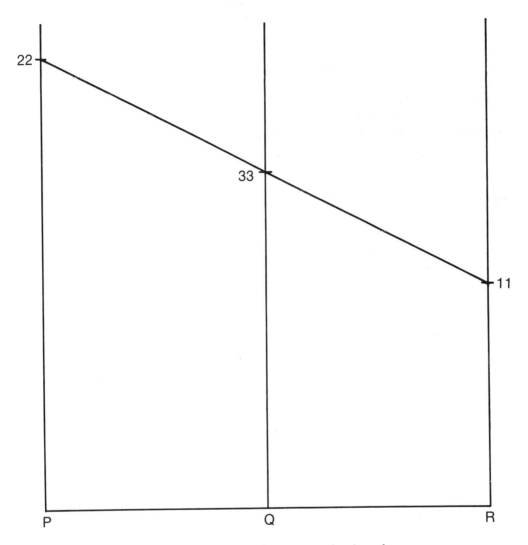

Figure 25. Adding on the nomograph — base 4.

The nomograph provides another device for reviewing the concepts developed in studying number bases other than ten after the unit has been completed.

AID FOURTEEN

NOMOGRAPH — MULTIPLICATION

In Aid Thirteen, we described a device for use when discussing the addition and subtraction of integers. After using this device, many students ask if there is a corresponding device for use in multiplication and division. This nomograph, based on the logarithmic formula that $\log AB = \log A + \log B$, provides some interest for all students, as well as an introduction to the principles of the slide rule for superior students.

MAKING THE NOMOGRAPH

This device is based on the slide rule C-scale. This is a logarithmic scale. On scales A and C, we use a standard scale (logarithmic scale). On the B-scale, we use a double logarithmic scale. This device should be prepared in advance on a duplication master, and distributed to the pupils.

USING THE NOMOGRAPH

The first half of the B-scale represents the integers from one to nine. The upper half of this B-scale represents the integers that are ten times the first ones (ten, twenty, thirty, etc.), from ten to one hundred. The pupils will have to estimate answers between these markings unless smaller units are put in in advance. This could be difficult in the small spaces between the upper numbers of the B-scale.

To find the product of two integers, (5)(4) for example, locate (5) on the A-scale and (4) on the C-scale. Connect these two points with a ruler, or draw a line. The product, 20, can be read on the B-scale, where the ruler (or line) crosses this scale.

Notice that to find the product of (8)(8), the line will cross the B-scale almost midway between the upper six and upper seven (60 and 70). This calls for the pupil to estimate the answer.

To use this Nomograph for division, locate the dividend on the B-scale, and the divisor on the A-scale. The quotient can be read on the C-scale.

Again, since estimated answers are necessary, this device cannot be used successfully with every class. It does, however, provide a good introduction to logarithms for second-year algebra students. They can calculate that the distance from one to two on the A and C scales is .301 of the entire scale (.301 = log 2); the distance from one to three on these scales is .477 of the entire length (log 3 = .477); this is true all the way up to log 10 = 1, the entire length of the A and C scales.

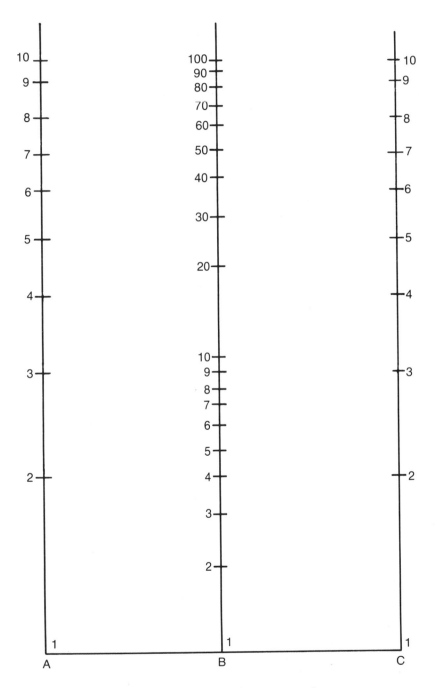

Figure 26. Multiplication nomograph.

AID FIFTEEN

MODEL FOR (a + b)²

Students in a beginning class in algebra often have trouble recognizing that the square of a binomial expression yields a trinomial expression. Most feel that there is a transitivity of an exponent over a sum. Thus, they often think that $(a + b)^2 = a^2 + b^2$, forgetting the middle term, 2ab. This device illustrates geometrically that this middle term is necessary.

MAKING THE MODEL

The model is made of posterboard or cardboard of various colors. A large piece of neutral colored posterboard is cut in the form of a square, ten inches on a side. This is divided by marks, three inches from each vertex. This gives a square with side (a + b) as shown.

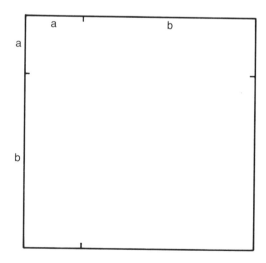

Figure 27. Base of square.

From a second piece of posterboard of another color, cut a square piece, three inches on a side. From another piece, cut a square that is seven inches on a side. From a fourth piece, cut two rectangles, each three inches wide by seven inches long.

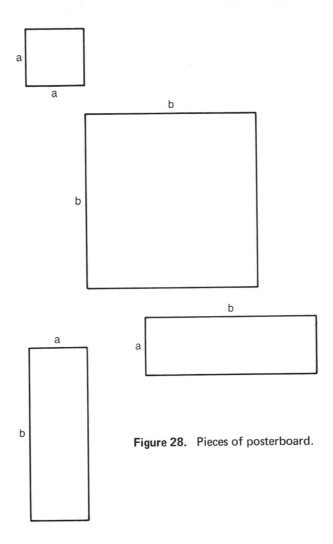

Figure 28. Pieces of posterboard.

These are hinged into position on the base square with cellophane tape, or masking tape. They are kept folded back until needed.

USING THE MODEL

1. The original model square is shown to the class, and a discussion of the meaning of $(a + b)^2$ should be held. It should be made clear to the students that $(a + b)^2$ means a square with side $(a + b)$.

The pieces that have been hinged into place are brought forward to their respective positions in front, and their areas discussed. Thus, the square of side a is put in place (area = a^2). The same is done with the square of side b (area = b^2). This will leave two rectangular pieces uncovered until, the two pieces, each of area ab, are put into place. The finished model will look like that in figure 29.

Figure 29. $(a + b)^2 = a^2 + b^2 + 2\,(ab)$.

PROBLEM SOLVING
— CARD GAME

When students are asked to name the one part of mathematics that causes them the most trouble, the answer usually given is problem solving. One possible reason for this reaction is that many students have trouble with the basic phrases that must be "translated" into correct mathematical expressions. This aid is a device to strengthen the students' introduction to this process, and increase his ability to use these key phrases correctly.

MAKING THE DECK

The deck consists of thirty-two cards, each approximately two and one-half inches by three inches. These can be made by cutting standard three inch by five inch file cards in half.

On each card, write or type one of the following phrases. At the bottom of the card, place an assigned point value, from one to five. The list that follows is only a suggested one; other phrases may be used as desired.

One point each

    (a) y increased by four

    (b) the sum of m and n

    (c) the product of k and w

    (d) s divided by t

    (e) the square of x

    (f) seven multiplied by p

    (g) two-thirds of y

Two points each

    (a) a less b

    (b) the sum of four y's

    (c) the difference between x and y

    (d) the quotient of 3a and 4b

    (e) five decreased by e

    (f) three times the product of m and n

    (g) twice x divided by four

Three points each

    (a) one-half increased by the product of three and x

    (b) three times the square of y

    (c) the square of (three multiplied by a)

    (d) the product of h and the square of k

    (e) a number increased by eight

    (f) eight less than some number, t

    (g) the difference between a number x and a number y

    (h) the difference between a number y and a number y

    (i) seven diminished by a number x

Four points each

    (a) the square of the sum of x and four

    (b) the sum of the squares of x and four

    (c) four added to twice an unknown quantity, x

    (d) twice an unknown quantity, x, diminished by seven

Five points each

    (a) the square of r minus the product of x and y

    (b) twice the product of the square of x and the square of y

    (c) the quotient of five times the square of w and four times the cube of y

    (d) the difference between the cube of x and the square of z

    (e) the excess of 10 over x

USING THE DECK

The class is divided into two teams. The cards are shuffled and mixed well. A card is turned over and the phrase and its point value are read aloud. The first student on one team is asked to give the answer. The answer may be given orally or written on the chalkboard. If he gives the correct mathematical expression, his team is credited with the stated number of points. If he misses, the first member of the other team tries. Play alternates in this manner until someone writes the phrase correctly. The next card is turned up, and play continues. The team with more points at the end of the game is the winner. The pack of cards may be used over and over.

In an alternate game, the entire class stands, and each student in turn tries a card. If he misses, he sits down and the next person tries the same card. Play continues until only one person remains, or all cards are used up.

AID SEVENTEEN

CONIC SECTIONS
—WAX PAPER FOLDING

One unusual and interesting approach to the conic sections is to have students construct them by means of the envelope of tangents to each curve. Any paper can be used for this; however, if common wax paper (found in any kitchen) is used as a medium, the clear distinct creases that this kind of paper forms when folded will form a clearly visible envelope to outline the curves and make them more pronounced. It is interesting to note that all the creases are straight lines, yet the envelopes form very distinct curved shapes.

MAKING THE FOLDINGS

1. The Parabola

Select a line segment, $\overline{AB}$ as the directrix. Choose a point, P, not on $\overline{AB}$, to serve as the focal point. Fold the paper so that point P coincides with any point on line segment $\overline{AB}$. Crease carefully. Now move point P to different position on $\overline{AB}$. Crease again. Continue this process until P has been made to coincide with many different points on $\overline{AB}$. The more creases, the sharper will be the outline of the parabola.

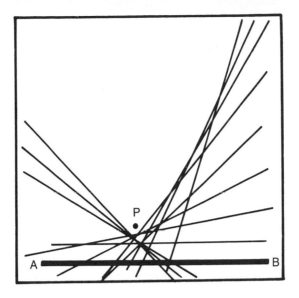

Figure 30. The parabola.

2. The Ellipse

Draw a circle with center at O. Select a point other than O, but also inside the circular region. Call this point P. The foci of the ellipse will be O and P. Fold the circle *without creasing* until point P coincides with a point on the circumference of the circle. Now crease carefully. Fold the circle so that P coincides with another point on the circumference. Crease again. Repeat the process until P has been made to coincide with many points along the circumference of the circle. The resulting creases should form the envelope of tangents that will describe the ellipse.

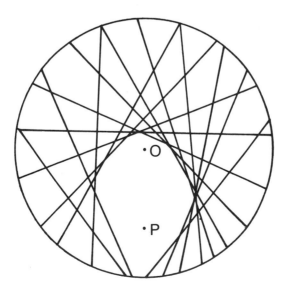

Figure 31. The ellipse.

3. The Hyperbola

Draw a circle with center at O. Select a point outside the circle, P. These points, O and P, will be the foci of the hyperbola. Fold the circle so that point P coincides with a point on the circumference of the circle. Crease carefully. Fold the circle so that P coincides with another point on the circumference. Crease again. Repeat this process until P has been made to coincide with many points along the circumference of the circle. The resulting creases will form the envelope of tangents that describe the hyperbola. Again, the more positions P has had along the circumference, the more clearly defined will be the branches of the hyperbola.

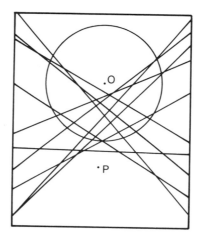

Figure 32. The hyperbola.

USING THE FOLDINGS

It may take some experimentation to locate point P (in reference to the circle) in such a position as to clearly define both branches of the hyperbola. This will depend upon the size of the radius of the circle, as well as how close to the circle we place point P. It may require several tries to obtain a satisfactory hyperbola.

When these curve foldings have been completed, they should be mounted on colorful construction paper. This background will accentuate the creases and the curve that has been outlined. The finished products make an excellent bulletin board display, as well as a series of models suitable for discussing the conic sections. Concepts such as the focus and directrix of a parabola and the foci of the ellipse and of the hyperbola are easily brought out in the process of the actual foldings of the envelopes of the tangents to the curves.

CURVE STITCHING

Curve stitching provides an interesting project that most classes enjoy. If approached carefully as a mathematics lesson (clearly devoid of any feminine connotations) the boys will participate eagerly and often they turn out some of the most creative ideas in the class. The pupils can make many intricate and original designs. Today's assortment of glowing colors, fluorescent pinks, greens, and oranges, for example, lend themselves to beautiful displays of curve stitching.

MAKING THE CURVES

The only equipment needed is an assortment of posterboard or other cardboard, for use as a background to sew on; a needle; and an assortment of brightly colored embroidery thread. Each student should be given materials to use as he alone wishes.

Many pupils need some guidance in the beginning. A good way to start is to draw a pair of lines that meet at about a sixty degree angle. Label the equally spaced units along one arm, with numerals from one to n, in consecutive order. Label in reverse order, from n to one, along the other arm.

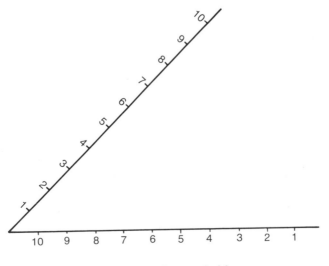

Figure 33. Curve stitching.

The student connects the same numbers on each arm; ie, join one to one, two to two, three to three, and so on, until n is joined to n. If a pupil runs out of thread in the middle of his work, he can both end the old thread and begin the new one by using cellophane tape on the back of his card. This avoids tying knots which inevitably come out. When the pupil has finished his work, he should have what appears to be a curve, even though every sewn line was a straight line. These lines form the envelope of the curve, in this case, the parabola.

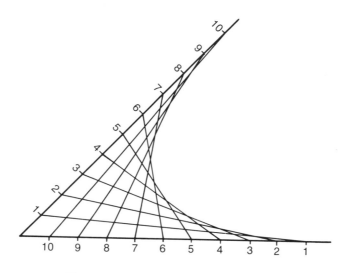

Figure 34. Curve stitching. The parabola.

Other possible curve stitching projects using the same general principles, might include:

(a) an equilateral triangle with a different colored parabola stitched into each angle,

(b) a "Z-shaped" trio of axes, with two stitchings, one inside each part of the "Z,"

(c) two perpendicular axes, forming the four quadrants. Stitch two parabolas inside each quadrant.

In another stitching project, we begin with a circle. Divide the circumference of the circle into thirty-six equally spaced points, labeled from one to thirty-six. If we join the point labeled one to the point labeled two, two to four, three to six, . . . n to 2n (or n to 2n − 36 once we reach nineteen), we obtain the mathematical curve, the *cardioid.*

If we begin the same way, but this time connect one to three, two to six, three to nine, . . . n to 3n (or n to 3n − 36 once we reach twelve), we obtain the *nephroid.*

Students might try this interesting arrangement: Draw two perpendicular diameters dividing a given circle into four quandrants. Mark each arc into equally spaced points, numbered from one to n. Mark each radius into equally spaced points, also labeled from one to n. Now, connect each point on an arc to the correspondingly labeled point on the nearest radius. Do this for each of the four quadrants. This same procedure can be followed for three equally spaced radii, five, or more.

If the pupils are left to use their own imaginations, they will design many attractive, original examples that make an excellent class display for a bulletin board or even a school showcase.

ALGEBRIDGE — CARD GAME

In the senior high schools, the students are far more sophisticated in their choice of games to play in a mathematics class. As a result, it is more difficult to develop a suitable card game, for say, an algebra class, than it might be for a junior high school arithmetic class. This card game, Algebridge, is one such possibility.

MAKING THE DECK

The deck consists of two parts, the *playing cards* and the *replacement* or value cards. The *playing cards,* fifty-two in all, should be made from oaktag or posterboard. Each should be about four inches long by two and one-half inches wide. The "suits" on the cards are indicated by using four colors — red, green, blue, and black are easily available in felt-tipped pens. On each card, print one of the following algebraic expressions:

$$(x^2 + 3x) \qquad (x^3 - 2x) \qquad (x^2) \qquad (x^3)$$

$$(2x^2 - 2x + 2) \qquad (x^4 - x^2 + 1) \qquad (x^3 + 2)$$

$$(7x - x^2) \qquad (x^3 + x^2 + 1) \qquad (4x - x^2)$$

$$(x^4 - 1) \qquad (\tfrac{1}{2}x^3) \qquad (x^3 + 7)$$

These same expressions (or any other preferred ones) are repeated in each suit, giving the fifty-two card playing deck.

The second part of the deck is a set of seventeen cards, the *replacement cards.* These are used to determine the replacement value for x during the play. This set consists of four cards with the numeral 4, four with the numeral 3, four with the numeral 2, four with the numeral 1, and one with the numeral 5. These cards are shuffled well, and kept separate from the playing cards.

USING THE DECK

The game is played similarly to bridge. There are four players. The *replacement set* is shuffled and placed face down in the center of the table. The *playing cards* are shuffled and dealt successively to each player until each has received thirteen cards. The player designated as North (by his seat) turns over the top *replacement card;* this is the value by which to replace the variable for that trick. (Note: a "trick" consists of one card played by each of the four players.) North now leads a card from any suit. All players must follow suit if they can; if they cannot, they may discard any card from their hand. However, if the card is not from the correct suit, it cannot win the trick. The winner of the trick is the player whose card has the highest value when x has been replaced by the value shown on the replacement card. It is now his turn to turn over the next value *replacement card* and lead a card. Play continues in this manner until all thirteen tricks are decided. The winning team is the one that wins most tricks.

STRATEGY GAMES — TOWER OF HANOI AND THE PEG GAME

An excellent way to reinforce a skill or a concept is to use some sort of mathematical game. Although most teachers prefer to use games that the entire class can participate in, some situations call for individual participation. However, in many cases, enough "game sets" can be made available so that the entire class can play, each pupil with a game of his own. These strategy games require the student to record his own work, gather his own data, and make his own generalizations under the teacher's guidance. Although there are many such games (the students probably all know how to play Tic-Tac-Toe for example), the Tower of Hanoi and the Peg Game are two excellent examples of these individual strategy games that can be used with an algebra class.

THE PEG GAME

Making the Game

The game consists of a playing surface with eleven congruent square regions.

Figure 35. The peg game — playing surface.

Colored pieces of construction paper (called FREEBELS) are used on this surface. If the square regions are large enough, coins can be used, such as dimes and pennies, or even small chips of two different colors. For illustration purposes, we shall represent the FREEBELS as:

Each student should receive a duplicated sheet with the playing surface on it, plus a set of ten FREEBELS, five of each color.

Using the Game

To begin the game, five red FREEBELS are placed in the five squares at one end of the playing surface, and five blue FREEBELS are placed in the five squares at the other end. The middle square region is left open.

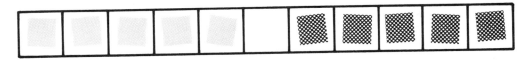

Figure 36. Peg game – starting position.

The object of the game is to interchange the positions of the red and blue FREEBELS in a minimum of moves. A FREEBEL can be moved in two ways:

(a) forward, from one square region to the adjacent one, or

(b) by "jumping" over a FREEBEL of the opposite color.

Moves backward are not allowed (it would no longer be a minimum number of moves if we reversed moves). Jumping a FREEBEL does not remove it from the playing surface.

After a suitable "frustration period," the teacher might suggest that the game be tried with one red FREEBEL and one blue FREEBEL. The playing surface should be set up this way:

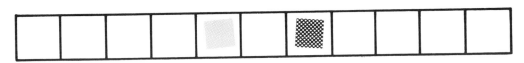

Figure 37. The peg game – one FREEBEL of each color.

The results can be tabulated as follows:

Number of red FREEBELS (p)	Number of moves required (n)

After the pupils have completed the game with one red and one blue FREEBEL, the game should be replayed with two red and two blue FREEBELS and the results should be recorded. The game should be played with three of each color, and then with four of each. The results will give the following pattern:

Number of red FREEBELS (p)	Number of moves required (n)
1	3
2	8
3	15
4	24
5	?

At the same time, a pattern of play should also emerge; this is to keep the FREEBELS in as much of an alternating color pattern as possible throughout the moves. The students should, on the basis of the collected data, then be asked to estimate the minimum number of moves for the full complement of five red FREEBELS. (The answer is 35.) They also should be encouraged to write a mathematical equation using p and n, where p = the number of red FREEBELS used and n = the minimum number of moves (the answer is $p^2 + 2p = n$ or $p(p + 2) = n$).

THE TOWER OF HANOI

Making the Game

This game consists of three "sticks" and a series of discs, or washers, of increasing size. The discs are placed in ascending size order on one of the three sticks.

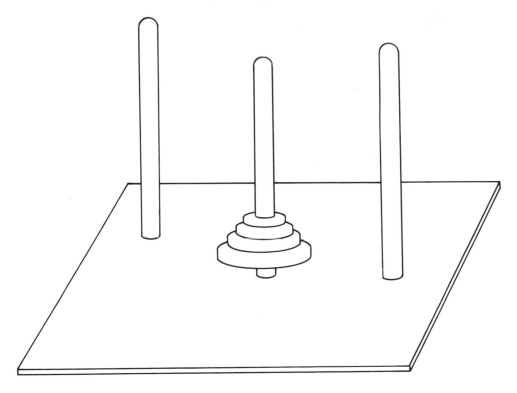

Figure 38. Tower of Hanoi.

USING THE GAME

The object of the game is to move the entire pile of discs from one stick to another. The moves are made in accordance with two rules:

(a) a larger disc can never be placed on top of a smaller disc, and

(b) only one disc at a time can be moved.

The game should again be played with two discs, then with three, four, and so on, and the results recorded in tabular form. In the first case, that of two discs, the required number of moves is three. When three discs are used, it requires seven moves to complete the game. After five discs, the table looks like this:

Number of Discs	Number of Moves
2	3
3	7
4	15
5	31
6	?

The class should be asked to figure out the number of moves required for six discs, for seven, and so forth. Is there any relationship between the number of discs and the number of moves? Is it related to the powers of two? This class discussion should lead to the expression $n = 2^p - 1$, where p is the number of discs used, and n the number of moves required.

Both these games, the Peg Game and the Tower of Hanoi, require students to concentrate. It is difficult to obtain a minimum number of moves quickly and without using exacting care.

Commercially made models of both of these games are readily available. It doesn't matter whether the games are homemade or purchased; they can be easily adapted to fit your own individual classroom situation.

SECTION THREE

GEOMETRY

DETERMINING THE VALUE OF PI

The number π has always fascinated mathematicians. For thousands of years they have been discovering methods for evaluating π. In the eighteenth century, Count Buffon used a needle method for finding an approximate value for π.

MAKING THE AID

A plane surface is ruled with a series of parallel lines each two having the same distance between them. Call this distance d. A needle is selected with its length either equal to d or less than d.

USING THE AID

The student stands above the ruled surface. He drops the needle onto the surface. A tally is kept of the number of times the needle falls on a line, as opposed to the number of times it falls between the lines. The ratio of the number of times the needle lands on a line to the number of times it lands between the lines will be an expression involving π. If the length of the needle being dropped is exactly one-half the distance between the lines (1/2d), then the ratio of total tosses to "successes" (a "success" is defined as the needle landing on a line) will be approximately π. The more tosses made, the closer will be the approximation to 3.14.

AID TWENTY-TWO

THE NAILBOARD — GEOBOARD

In most introductory courses in intuitive geometry, we want our students to discover some of the relationships that exist between geometric figures. The pupils should be given a supply of rubber bands and then should be turned loose to make and investigate any figures they wish.

MAKING THE BOARD

Make the geoboard from a piece of plywood, one-quarter of an inch thick. It should be about twenty inches long by twenty inches wide for a class demonstration model. A smaller piece of the same wood can be used to make individual student models. If the surface of the plywood is darkly colored or marred, it should be painted with a light color paint for background.

Drive small, headless nails (brads) into the board in a pattern of small squares, approximately one inch apart. This should give the board a graph grid-like appearance.

USING THE BOARD

Supply each pupil (or group of pupils) with a number of rubber bands of varying size. Allow the pupils to experiment with the board for a while. Do not let this initial experimentation time drag; it leads to boredom and flying rubber bands.

Pose a series of challenging questions to the students and let them work individually or in pairs. The questions could be duplicated ahead of time. Some suitable problems might include the following:

(a) Use a rubber band to make a 5 x 5 square. Within that square, how many different sized squares can you make? If your answer is four counting the original 5 x 5 square, keep on looking. There are more.

(b) Make a figure having a perimeter of 12 units. Make another figure also having a perimeter of 12 units. Do these two figures contain the same area? On your geoboard, make a figure with a perimeter of 12 units, and having the largest area possible. Make a figure with a perimeter of 12 units, and having the smallest area possible.

Encourage the students to make up questions similar to these and to share them with the other students in the class.

Notice that the use of the one inch squares on the geoboard allows measurement to play a significant role in the experiments if the teacher so desires. It is not necessary to use this idea, however, when discussing the general properties of geometric figures.

AID TWENTY-THREE

CIRCLEBOARD

When students study the many theorems in the unit on circles in a course in geometry, they often have trouble visualizing the many relationships that exist between the multitude of lines and line segments both inside and outside the circle. The circleboard will enable each student to see these relationships first-hand using rubber bands to represent the line segments.

The circleboard whose construction is described here is one to be used by the teacher as a demonstration model in front of a class, or small group. However, the students themselves can construct one for each pupil, by using a scale approximately one-half that given in the following description.

MAKING THE CIRCLEBOARD

Take a piece of plywood one-quarter inch thick. It should be about twenty inches long by twenty inches wide. If the surface is dark or discolored, the board should be painted a light color to make it easily visible in the back of the room. On the board, paint a circle with a six inch radius. Do *not* center the circle on the board. Drive small, headless wire brads around the circumference at about half-inch intervals. Leave about one-half of each brad sticking up from the surface. Drive several extra brads into different positions outside the circle as well as one brad directly in the center of the circle.

USING THE CIRCLEBOARD

The students should be given a supply of rubber bands. These can be stretched over the brads to make radii, diameters, and chords of the circle. Tangents and secants can also be made using the outside brads. These "lines" can be carefully examined for relationships, or measured for length by the students using rulers, protractors, and other means. In this manner, pupils can "discover" for themselves what relationships exist within these lines and the related circle.

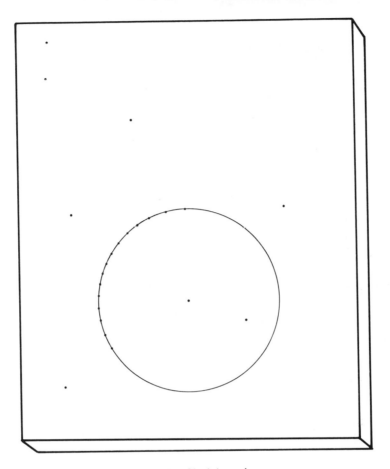

Figure 39. Circleboard.

THE TRIANGLE
—WAX PAPER FOLDING

In the typical introductory course in geometry as taught in the junior high schools, a major emphasis is put upon a thorough investigation of the triangle, its properties, and the line segments associated with it. Instead of having the teacher develop these ideas with the students as spectators, it is easy to involve each child if he has his own triangles to experiment with.

MAKING THE TRIANGLES

Although any kind of paper can be used, ordinary kitchen-style wax paper is excellent for all kinds of foldings. Cut a series of triangles of all shapes and sizes from a sheet of this paper, or any other paper. Another possibility is to have each pupil bring a set of triangles that he has cut out in advance as a homework assignment. "Any size or shape" should be emphasized; the more varied, the better for the general conclusions of the discovery.

USING THE TRIANGLES

A good beginning theorem to "discover" is that the sum of the measures of the angles of any triangle is exactly one straight angle.

1. Each student holds his own triangle in the same standard position, with vertex C at the top.

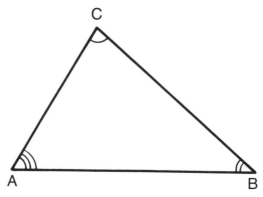

Figure 40-A.

2. Fold vertex C so that it falls on line segment AB, directly underneath C.

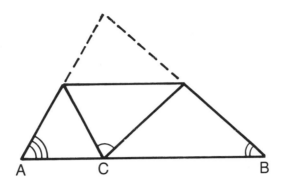

Figure 40-B.

3. Now fold vertex A to meet point C and vertex B to meet point C.

4. The three angles will have their sides in the positions shown, demonstrating the theorem, since $\overline{ACB}$ can be viewed as a straight angle with vertex at C.

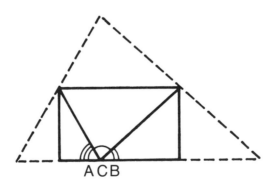

Figure 40-C.

Another interesting "discovery" for pupils to make is the fact that the three angle bisectors of angles A, B, and C are concurrent.

1. Hold the triangle in the standard position as described above.

2. Fold, so that segment $\overline{AC}$ falls along segment $\overline{BC}$. Crease carefully.

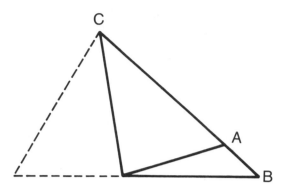

Figure 41. Folding the angle bisectors.

3. Unfold. There should be a clearly defined line segment, the angle bisector of angle C.

4. Repeat the same procedure. Make segment $\overline{BC}$ fall along segment $\overline{AB}$. Unfold. Then repeat a third time, making segment $\overline{AC}$ fall along segment $\overline{AB}$.

5. If we now examine the three creases that define the angle bisectors of the three angles of the triangle, we can clearly demonstrate that all three intersect in one common point within the triangle.

The same procedure may be followed to investigate the concurrency of the altitudes and of the medians. In the case of the three medians, we first locate the midpoint of segment $\overline{AB}$ by holding vertex A on top of vertex B and creasing slightly at this midpoint, M. Then, we fold a line segment from vertex C to this new point, M. If we unfold, we have $\overline{CM}$, the median from C to AB. Now repeat this process to obtain the medians to sides BC and AC. These three medians should be concurrent within the triangular region.

In the case of the altitudes, slide vertex A along segment AB until the crease line just passes through vertex C. Crease carefully.

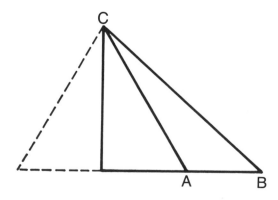

Figure 42. Folding the altitudes.

When we unfold, we should have the altitude to side $\overline{AB}$. Do the same to obtain the altitudes to sides $\overline{BC}$ and $\overline{AC}$. When we unfold the altitudes should be concurrent. However, a word of explanation is due here. If the original triangle selected was scalene, acutc, then the altitudes will be concurrent within the triangular region. If the triangle was a right triangle, then the altitudes will be concurrent *on the vertex of the right angle*. If the original triangle was an obtuse triangle, then the altitudes will not appear to be concurrent. However, if the triangle is pasted onto a piece of paper and the altitudes extended, they will be concurrent, *outside the triangle*. This should be carefully explained to the pupils while they are working on the project.

The finished work of the students can be mounted on colorful construction paper. These will then provide an excellent bulletin board display for the classroom.

AID TWENTY-FIVE

AREA COMPUTER

An introduction to the area of a polygon is something that is often passed over rather quickly in the introductory courses in geometry. In many cases, the pupils do not fully comprehend what we mean by a region containing so many "square units." This aid is to provide these pupils with a concrete representation of what area means.

MAKING THE AREA COMPUTER

The board consists of a piece of plywood, one-eighth of an inch thick. It should be about thirty inches long by thirty inches wide. This should be covered with a brightly colored piece of felt. A color such as blue or green or red would be excellent. The board is then marked off into small squares with pieces of white yarn. A square that is one and one-half inches on a side is a good size. The various polygonal shapes are then made from ordinary soda straws. These are cut to the desired lengths with a scissors, and fastened with brass fasteners.

USING THE AREA COMPUTER

The students should discuss what is meant by a square unit. The squares on the board can be carefully counted, and the area of the board computed in square units.

A rectangle or square made from the straws should then be placed on the board. The number of square blocks it encloses can be counted. Moving the figure around, turning it upside down, and so forth will enable the students to see that the number of square units it contains does not change.

If we now place a triangle on the board and compute its area (approximately), we can change the size and shape of the triangle with no change in its perimeter. The students can actually *see* this change in area taking place.

AREA OF A CIRCULAR REGION

The area of a circular region is something that many teachers find difficult to present to students in an intuitive course in geometry. The concept of π is difficult, and the students often have some trouble understanding the area of a circle in terms of π. This aid, while informal and only approximate, is quite useful as an introduction to the area formula. It depends upon the pupils' knowing the formulae for the circumference of a circle and the area of a parallelogram.

MAKING THE AID

1. A circle is drawn either on posterboard or on one-eighth inch thick plywood. This circle is then divided into a number of pie-shaped wedges — sectors — as shown:

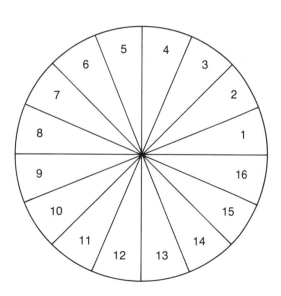

Figure 43. Area of circular region.

2. After discussing the formula for the circumference of this circle, (C = 2πr), in terms of its radius, r, the circle is then taken apart into the wedge-shaped sections.

3. These sectors are then arranged in alternating positions as shown:

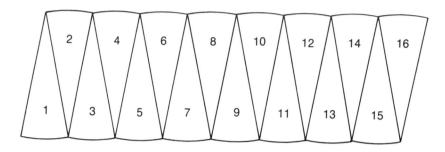

Figure 44.   Area of circular region.

4. The figure now approximates a parallelogram. The more sectors, the more closely the figure will be to a parallelogram. The base of this "parallelogram" is one-half the circumference; the altitude is the same length as the radius of the original circle. Thus the area of the circular region approximates the area of the "parallelogram":

$$A = b \times h$$

$$A = (\tfrac{1}{2}C)\ (r)$$

$$A = (\tfrac{1}{2})\ (2\pi r)\ (r)$$

$$A = \pi r^2$$

A SIMPLE LINKAGE — AN ANGLE

In courses in geometry, the basic figure most discussed between pupils and teachers is the angle. Many concepts are discussed, with the usual procedure being the chalk-talk, lecture kind of lesson. The angle is usually drawn on the chalkboard. In doing this, the teacher sometimes loses the dynamic properties of the angle. This aid is a simple linkage designed to add this dimension to the study of the angle. A linkage is so-called because it is made by "linking" or joining two pieces of wood or posterboard together, so that motion is possible.

MAKING THE ANGLE LINKAGE

From a piece of posterboard, oaktag, or some other firm material, cut two strips, each about one-half inch in width and twelve inches in length. Attach the two pieces of posterboard at one end, to form an angle. Use a brass fastener at the vertex to do this.

USING THE ANGLE LINKAGE

This angle linkage may be used to illustrate the different kinds of angles — obtuse, right, acute, straight, and reflex — by holding one side of the linkage in place, and moving the other side. The point should be carefully developed that the number of degrees in the measure of an angle has nothing to do with the lengths of the sides. In fact, one side can be made shorter than the other to show that the lengths of the sides need not even be the same in an angle.

The angle can now be fixed into one position by tightening the brass fastener at the vertex. An acute angle is best for this. The lengths of the sides of the angle should now be cut off, piece by piece. After each cut, the class should be made to realize that the number of degrees in the measure of the angle has not changed at all. If a chalkboard protractor is available, students can actually measure the number of degrees in the measure of the angle at the various stages of cutting the sides.

THE PANTOGRAPH — LINKAGES

The artist's tool that enables him to easily enlarge or shrink a drawing is the pantograph. This is a commonly used device, and a commercially manufactured model is easily obtainable at any commercial art supply store. It is relatively easy to make, however, as a simple linkage. The exercise is a valuable one, and provides material for a discussion on similarity in a geometry class.

MAKING THE PANTOGRAPH

Strips of heavy posterboard are excellent for making this device. Brass fasteners work well for fastening the strips together to form the linkage. For the pantograph, cut four strips of posterboard, each about one inch wide. Two of the strips should be twelve inches in length (these are AC and FC in the figure); the other two should each be six inches in length (BE and DE in the figure).

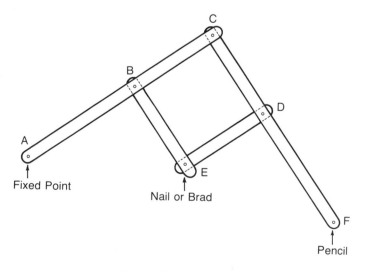

Figure 45. A pantograph.

Fasten the strips of posterboard as shown in the figure. It is important that BCDE always be a parallelogram. It is not necessary to use the 2:1 ratio suggested in this illustration. The brass fasteners will allow the entire assembled linkage to move at the joints.

USING THE PANTOGRAPH

When using the pantograph to enlarge a picture or a drawing, keep point A fixed. Use a thumbtack to do this. Place a pencil through a hole made at point F. Push a small brad or nail through point E; this will serve as a tracing point.

After fixing point A, place a fresh sheet of paper underneath point F. Place the drawing to be copied underneath the nail at point E. Move the nail along the drawing slowly. The pencil at F will make an enlarged drawing of the picture being traced at E.

AID TWENTY-NINE

BALLOON SPHERE

In a geometry class, we discuss the properties of spherical triangles, and often an entire unit of geometry on a sphere. In many cases, the teacher either draws two-dimensional representations of these three-dimensional figures on a chalkboard, or uses an overhead projector with drawings and pictures that are still two-dimensional. Sometimes, we use a spherical chalkboard if one is available. This aid has great "shock" value, as well as being a simple model for this interesting unit.

MAKING THE MODEL

1. In any variety store, purchase a large sphere-shaped balloon. A solid yellow color is one of the best to use. The larger the better, providing it is easily inflated and is strong.

2. Inflate the balloon to the maximum size desired. Do this before showing it to the class. If the balloon is inflated and deflated a few times, it will be easier to inflate rapidly in class.

3. With a permanent, nylon-tipped pen, draw the desired spherical triangle or polygon on the surface of the inflated balloon. Polar triangles can also be drawn.

4. Allow the figure to dry thoroughly before deflating the balloon.

USING THE MODEL

Since one purpose of any aid is to create interest in the topic under discussion, keep the balloon in a pocket or in a drawer of the desk until it is needed. At an appropriate point in the discussion, take out the balloon, inflate it to the proper size, and begin discussing the spherical polygons which will appear on it.

The balloon can be inflated or deflated a little without any loss of accuracy in the drawings on it. This will allow for a discussion of congruency in spherical terminology.

"RIFFLE BOOK" — LOCUS

One approach to the topic of *locus* in geometry study is to approach it as the path of a moving point tracing a geometric figure as it moves. Unfortunately, the pupils rarely "see" the point actually moving, unless a movie is shown. The riffle book approach can change this, and each pupil can make his own "moving point."

MAKING THE BOOK

1. Each "book" consists of between ten and twenty small cards. Ordinary three inch by five inch file cards are excellent for this.

2. As an example, let us look at the locus theorem, "The locus of points equidistant from the ends of a line segment is the perpendicular bisector of that line segment."

3. Every card has the line segment ($\overline{AB}$) drawn on it in the same position. On card number one, place the point that will "move" in starting position.

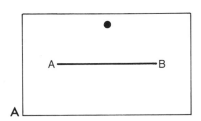

4. On the next card, place the point in a position *slightly* moved — along the path of the locus — from its position on the first card.

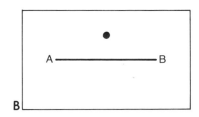

5. Continue this procedure throughout all the cards until the last card shows the point in its final position along the path of the locus.

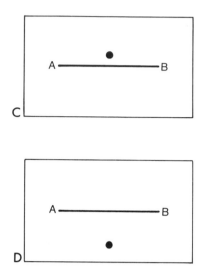

Figure 46. "Riffle book — locus."

6. Clip all the cards together in *order* with one clip or fastener in the upper left hand corner.

USING THE BOOK

After discussing the locus theorems at hand, the students hold the riffle book in the corner where the cards are clipped together. He flips through the cards as rapidly as possible, trying not to skip any of the cards. His eye should retain the image of the point (which should be quite dark and pronounced) as he flips through the book, long enough for him to "see" the point move and describe the given locus.

Some good locus theorems for riffle books might include:

(a) the locus of the vertex of a right angle with fixed hypotenuse is a semi-circle with the hypotenuse as diameter;

(b) the locus of points equidistant from the sides of an angle is the bisector of the angle;

(c) the locus of points equidistant from two parallel lines is a third line, parallel to the two given lines, and midway between them.

MODELS OF THE REGULAR POLYHEDRONS

One of the many skills teachers try to develop in a spatial geometry course is the ability of the pupil to discover and express relationships that he finds when working with solid figures. Unfortunately, the textbooks can only show two-dimensional pictures of the three-dimensional figures. As a result, the student often cannot find the results he is seeking. These models of the five regular polyhedrons, tetrahedron, cube (hexahedron), octahedron, dodecahedron, and icosahedron, are easy to construct. They are made up of plane geometry figures with which the students should be familiar.

MAKING THE MODELS

The patterns shown can be prepared in advance on a ditto master by the teacher, or can be copied by the students onto graph paper. If the teacher prepares them in advance, they can be duplicated on colorful art paper, rather than plain graph paper. The models should then be cut carefully along the solid lines. They should be carefully creased and folded along the dotted lines, and taped into place with cellophane tape.

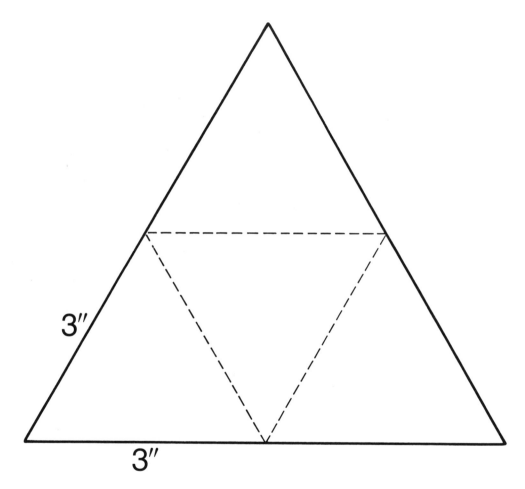

Figure 47. Regular tetrahedron.

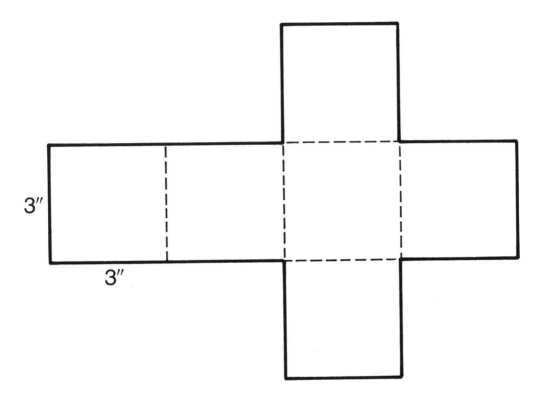

Figure 48. Regular hexahedron (cube).

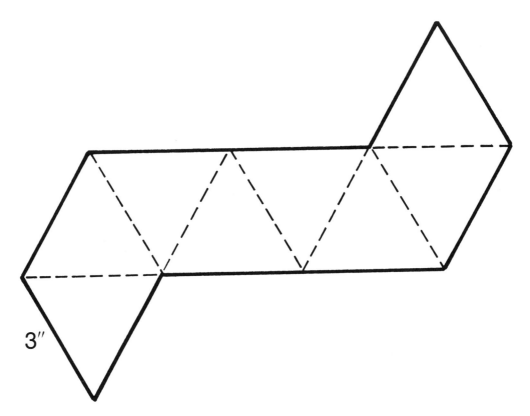

Figure 49. Regular octahedron.

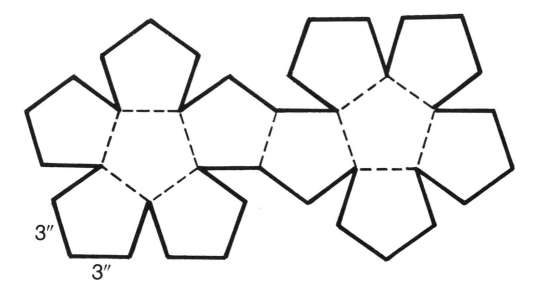

Figure 50. Regular dodecahedron.

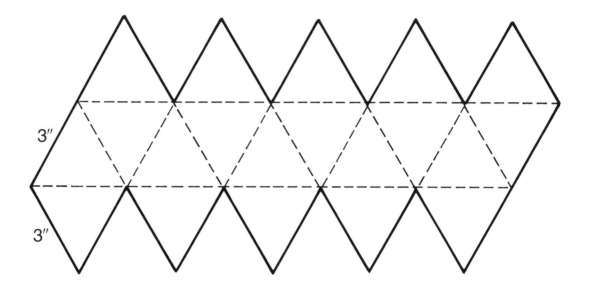

Figure 51. Regular icosahedron.

USING THE MODELS

After the students have made their own sets of polyhedrons, they should try to complete the following table, and try to find a mathematical equation using F, V and E, where F is the number of faces, V is the number of vertices, and E is the number of edges. (The answer is F + V = E + 2, which is known by mathematicians as Euler's Law.)

Figure	Number of Faces F	Number of Vertices V	Number of Edges E
tetrahedron			
cube			
octahedron			
dodecahedron			
icosahedron			

An interesting show-type of project is to make the models in different sizes and on different kinds of paper as well. Gift wrapping paper makes beautiful models. When these models are completed, they can be strung with black thread and hung from a wire clothes hanger to make a set of Mathmobiles to suspend around the classroom.

CHINESE TANGRAM PUZZLE

Probably one of the oldest mechanical puzzles is the ancient Chinese tangram puzzle. It has been known in the Orient for several thousand years. The name, tangram, however, is a mid-nineteenth century name, coined by some American or British toy manufacturer. It has been said that Napoleon spent much of the time while in exile working on this puzzle. There are many books of tangram solutions available; some of them are quite recent. This verifies the continuous and ongoing popularity of this little puzzle.

The idea of dissection puzzles has always intrigued mathematicians. David Hilbert, for example, showed that if two figures of equal area are dissected in the proper manner, each can be reconstructed in the shape of the other one. These dissection puzzles provide a great deal of work with spatial relationships in introductory courses in geometry. The students are encouraged to use their imaginations; they often devise unique solutions and puzzles. It is a good idea to keep a record of the many shapes the pupils devise; it encourages original thought and competition.

MAKING THE TANGRAMS

A large square is cut as shown in figure 52.

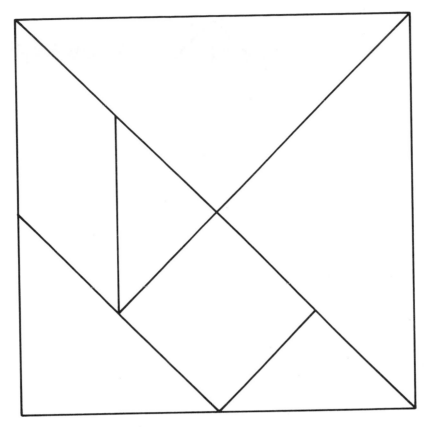

Figure 52. The seven tangram pieces.

These seven pieces form the tangram set. This can be prepared on a ditto master and run off on posterboard or cardboard for each pupil to make his own set. Some students may wish to make a more permanent set out of one-eighth inch thick plywood on their own. The pieces should be the same color on both sides, since they can be turned over if desired. Each pupil can keep his own set of tangram pieces in an envelope.

USING THE TANGRAMS

Each student should have his own set of tangram pieces so that he can work along with the teacher. The basic rule of the tangram puzzle is that all seven pieces must be used in each dissection.

The teacher might begin by challenging the class to assemble their tangram pieces into some familiar geometric shape such as the triangle. After the pupils have worked at it for a time, the teacher can reveal the solution. An overhead projector is excellent for this unit.

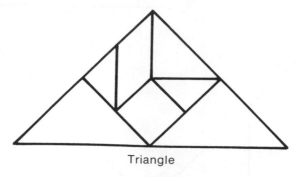

Triangle

Figure 53.

As a next step, the class might be asked to make a tangram figure of a Chinese Coolie bowing. Again, the solution should not be revealed until the pupils have had an appropriate length of time to try to figure the puzzle out.

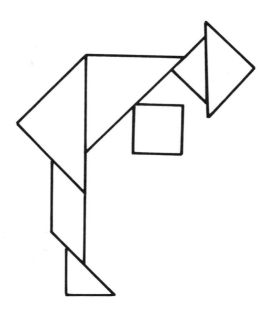

Figure 54.   Chinese coolie bowing.

Since the pupils will finish these figures at different individual rates, the teacher might post many other figures around the room.

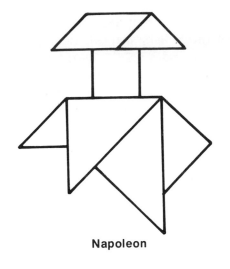

Napoleon

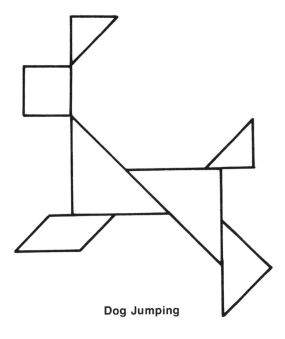

Scotch Terrier

Dog Jumping

Figure 55.

Whenever a student finishes some other work, he can get his set of tangram pieces and try some of these. If he makes a figure, his name is placed on the sheet with that figure as a record.

The teacher might also allow the students to develop their own figures. These results can be recorded in a class notebook as a permanent record. They can also be duplicated, collated, and given to each student as a challenge book of his own.

POLYOMINOES

In 1954, Solomon W. Golomb introduced the term *polyominoes* in an article that he wrote for the *American Mathematical Monthly* magazine. He defined polyominoes as simply connected sets of congruent squares. Most students have seen or used dominoes (two congruent squares, simply connected); they comprehend the single, rectangular shape that the domino must be. It is possible to discuss trominoes (figures made up of three, congruent, simply connected squares) and to illustrate the two shapes possible. Tetrominoes, four congruent squares, have only five possible arrangements.

When we get to the pentominoes, however, there are twelve possible arrangements of the five congruent squares. Many geometric relationships can be discussed using these pentominoes.

MAKING THE PENTOMINOES

It is a good idea to have the pupils discuss the trominoes and tetrominoes before beginning the pentominoes. The class should be asked to sketch the shapes on a piece of graph paper and place them on the board. When all twelve have been discovered by the pupils, the teacher can distribute a set that has been duplicated in advance and run off on oaktag or some other kind of light cardboard. Each student can then cut out his own set of pentominoes.

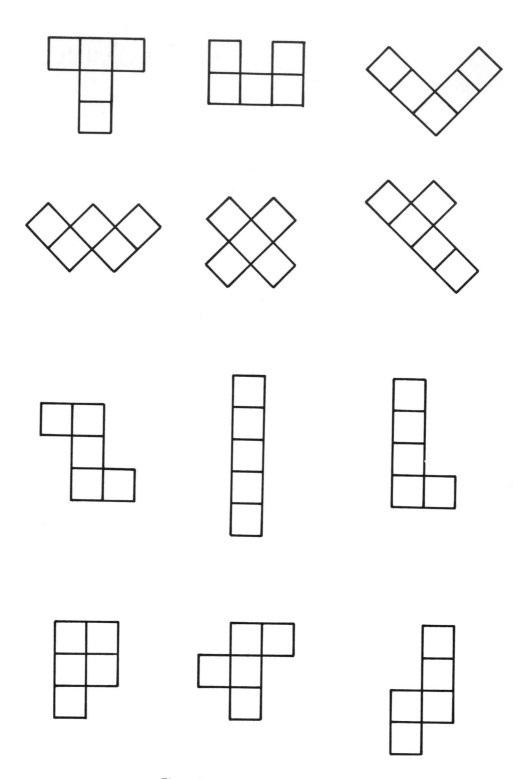

Figure 56.   The twelve pentominoes.

USING THE PENTOMINOES

A simple way to have the students begin, is to ask them to arrange the pentominoes into a set of rectangles. If we make the pentominoes from one inch squares, we can refer to the rectangles in terms of inches, rather than units. There are supposed to be over two thousand ways to arrange the pieces into a six by ten rectangle:

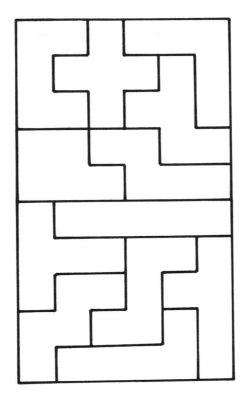

Figure 57-A.

Notice that this six by ten rectangle can be broken up into two rectangles, each five by six. These same two rectangles can then be reassembled into a five by twelve rectangle.

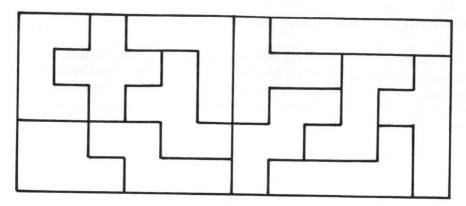

Figure 57-B.

We can also ask the students to arrange the pentominoes into a four by fifteen rectangle and a three by twenty rectangle.

There are many other ideas that can be utilized with a class and a set of twelve pentominoes. An excellent source for this material (other than Golomb's original article) is in the works of Martin Gardner. In both SCIENTIFIC AMERICAN BOOK OF MATHEMATICAL PUZZLES AND DIVERSIONS (Simon and Schuster, 1959) and MARTIN GARDNER'S NEW MATHEMATICAL DIVERSIONS FROM SCIENTIFIC AMERICAN (Simon and Schuster, 1966), Mr. Gardner devotes extensive sections to this topic.

SECTION FOUR

TRIGONOMETRY

CLINOMETER
— VERTICAL PROTRACTOR

When a course in trigonometry (or even a unit on trigonometry in a geometry course) is presented to students, the idea of indirect measurement and surveying is often presented and stressed. Yet few or no actual experiments with the students really measuring a school flagpole or building, or laying out a tennis court, for example, are ever carried out. Sometimes the reason is the teacher's unfamiliarity with surveying instruments. This aid and the ones that follow can easily be made by the pupils. They can then be used for experiments in elementary surveying.

MAKING THE CLINOMETER

Each student should have a rectangular piece of posterboard, oaktag, or cardboard about eight and one-half inches by eleven inches in size. Place a protractor in the corner of the posterboard as shown.

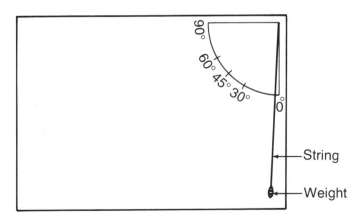

Figure 58. The clinometer.

The protractors can be drawn by the pupils directly on the posterboard, or can be duplicated in advance by the teacher and then be pasted on. It need only go from 0 degrees to 90 degrees for this aid. At the vertex of the protractor-angle, attach a plumb line made from a piece of string with a small weight attached. A large paper clip will usually suffice.

USING THE PROTRACTOR

1. Because of the weight attached, the string will always remain in a vertical position. This will enable the students to read the angle of elevation of the top of the building being measured directly from their clinometer.

2. The pupils should work in crews of three or four pupils. Have the students use the device and sight along the top of it, locating the top of the building, T, in our diagram. The angle shown here is a 50 degree angle, read by another pupil from the clinometer.

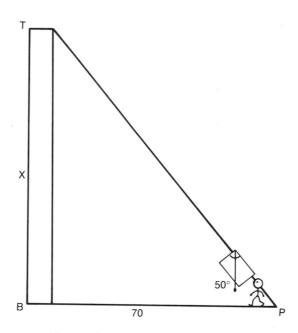

Figure 59.   Using the clinometer.

3. Another student should measure the distance from the student with the clinometer to the base of the building (BP). In our picture, this is seventy feet.

4. When the class has measured this data, the experiment can be taken back to the classroom and reduced to the following diagram:

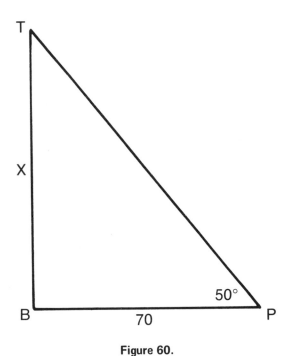

Figure 60.

5. Some computation with a table of tangent values will enable the students to compute the actual height of the building. Notice that the distance from the ground to the eye level of the students has been ignored in the calculations. The teacher can adjust the diagram as he sees fit.

THE ANGLE MIRROR

Another measuring device that lends itself well to outdoor work in classes of students in trigonometry is the *angle mirror.* This device, easily made, is used exclusively for obtaining right angles in construction work. Tennis courts, corners of buildings, swimming pools, and so forth, are all carefully laid out with the aid of the angle mirror.

MAKING THE MIRROR

The materials needed for making an angle mirror are two small dime-store mirrors, two small blocks of wood, and one piece of wood as a base, about eight inches long by eight inches wide. There is no need for large mirrors; they can easily become too unwieldy. For this angle mirror, dime-store mirrors about one to two inches on a side are sufficient.

Begin by gluing a small rectangular block of wood to the back of each of the mirrors. These blocks are then mounted on the base piece of wood with small screws. The mirrors should be carefully mounted at a 45 degree angle. This is easily obtained by folding the corner of a sheet of paper in half, or simply by using a protractor accurately. When the angle mirror is completed, a handle can be added for ease in holding it.

USING THE MIRROR

It must be kept in mind that the angle mirror only serves one purpose, namely, to make a right angle on the ground. It is best used by students in a group, as are most of these rough surveying instruments.

To use the mirror, a student at point L in Figure 62 looks at an object at point M. He looks into the mirror at the same time.

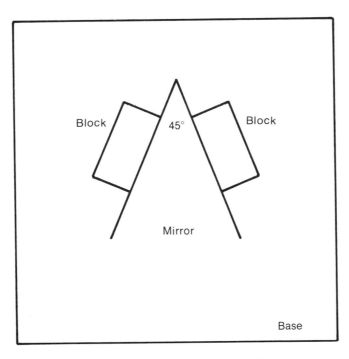

Figure 61. Angle mirror – top view.

Through double reflection, he can see the object at point O. It is advisable to use a student at O, since he can be directed to move to either side as needed merely by hand motions. In this way the student with the mirror "lines up" visually in the mirror, point O with his actual sighting of point M. When he does this, angle MNO will be twice the angle of the mirror, and therefore, 90 degrees. If we insert a plumb line at the edge of the board on which the angle mirror is mounted, we can quite accurately mark the vertex of the right angle.

After a little practice, an excellent exercise is to have each group of pupils lay out a rectangle on the ground.

Have the students mark off line segment PQ on the ground with string. The student with the mirror stands at point P.

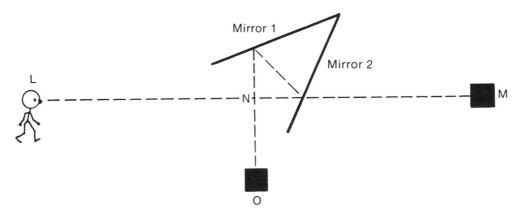

Figure 62. Using the mirror.

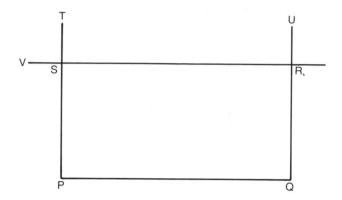

Figure 63. "Sighting" a rectangle.

He looks at another pupil at point Q. He sights a student at point T with the angle mirror, directing this student until students Q and T can be "seen" together in the mirror and line of sight. A string is then stretched from P to T. The process is repeated by another member of the group standing at point Q, then point U is located, and a string is stretched there. Point S is arbitrarily marked off along string PT. The process is repeated to establish the right angle at PSR, completing the rectangle. If a pupil looks out of a second story window, he can see if the rectangle has been correctly laid out.

THE CENTROMETER

When doing elementary surveying, it is sometimes necessary to find the center of a circular object before driving stakes into the ground. Since the center of a circle lies along the perpendicular bisector of any chord, we can make a simple instrument for finding the center of a circle by utilizing this concept.

MAKING THE CENTROMETER

Although this instrument can be made from posterboard, it is better cut from one-eighth inch thick plywood if possible. The handle can be made from a six inch piece of broomstick or heavy dowel, and fastened to the centrometer, or the entire instrument can be made from one piece. The important thing is that $\overline{AB}$ be perpendicular to $\overline{CD}$, and that segment $\overline{BC}$ be the same length as segment $\overline{BD}$. If the centrometer is made from wood, drive two small brads through points C and D.

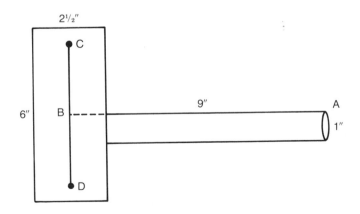

Figure 64. Centrometer.

USING THE CENTROMETER

In order to find the center of a circular object, slide the centrometer so that the two nails at C and at D just touch the circumference of the object. Now draw a line segment along $\overline{AB}$. Move the centrometer to a second position and draw another line. These two lines will be the diameters of the circle. Their intersection will be point O, the center of the circle.

THE TOMAHAWK TRISECTOR

Somewhere during his exposure to mathematics in secondary school, every student hears about the impossibility of trisecting an angle, under Euclidean conditions. Many of these same pupils often ask whether there is any instrument designed especially for performing this trisection problem. This homemade instrument, the tomahawk trisector, is used quite often in surveying and in measuring, whenever trisection is important. It is another easily made instrument that can be applied to outdoor experiments in surveying by a class.

MAKING THE TOMAHAWK TRISECTOR

The tomahawk can be made from heavy posterboard, cardboard, or plywood. It is similar to the standard carpenter's square. As shown in the figure, it is made by drawing a semi-circular disc, with any arbitrary radius, r.

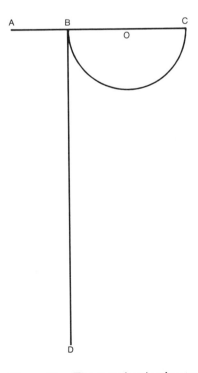

Figure 65. The tomahawk trisector.

The diameter, $\overline{BOC}$, is extended through B to point A, another radius in length, so that $\overline{AB} = \overline{BO} = \overline{OC} = r$. $\overline{BD}$ is a tangent to circle O at B, and thus it is also perpendicular to diameter $\overline{ABC}$. A handy length for $\overline{BD}$ is about five or six times the length of the radius, r. Wooden braces may be added in order to make the tomahawk a rigid instrument.

USING THE TOMAHAWK TRISECTOR

Suppose we wish to trisect an angle such as angle QRS:

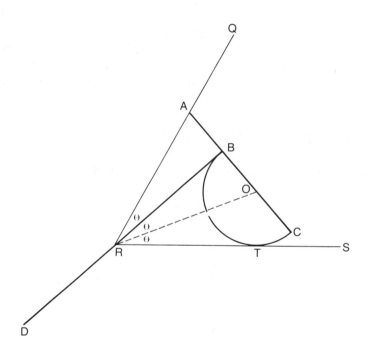

Figure 66.   Using the tomahawk.

Place the tomahawk so that point A is on one side of the angle. Now slide the device until $\overline{BD}$ passes through the vertex, R. At the same time, the semi-circle should be made tangent to the other side of the angle (point T). Then the points B and O together with R determine the trisection of angle QRS.

The proof of this trisection rests on the fact that right triangles ARB, ORB, and ORT are all congruent.

SPHEROMETER

In courses in trigonometry and spatial geometry, we are often interested in measuring the diameter of some spherical object. A class can make this simple device as another project, and then use it to measure the diameter of some spherical object such as a ball, for example. Again, the discussion behind the similar triangles and the proportions involved in this aid yields a very informative class session.

MAKING THE SPHEROMETER

The materials needed for this device are a cylinder open at one end (a coffee can), with a hole in the center of the closed end and a ruler or a calibrated dowel.

Insert the ruler or dowel through the hole in one end of the can. Be sure that the hole is wide enough to allow the stick to move up and down freely through the hole in the end.

USING THE SPHEROMETER

Place the open end of the cylinder over the sphere whose diameter is to be computed.

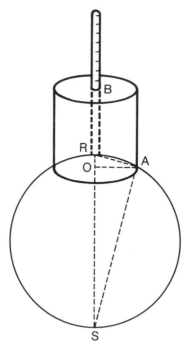

Figure 67. Spherometer.

The ruler will indicate the height of that part of the sphere that is inside the can. Since the height of the tin can, $\overline{OB}$, is known, the radius of the can is known, $\overline{OA}$, and we can compute the height of the part of the sphere in the cylinder, $\overline{OR} = \overline{OB} - \overline{RB}$, we are able to compute the diameter of the sphere by using the proportion:

$$\frac{OS}{OA} = \frac{OA}{OR}$$

This will give us segment $\overline{OS}$. When this is obtained, we find the diameter of the sphere = $\overline{OR} + \overline{OS}$.

SECTION FIVE

MISCELLANEOUS

THE MOBIUS STRIP

An adjunct field to the geometry studied in secondary schools is that of topology. An entertaining introduction to this relatively new field in mathematics can be provided for students with the mobius band or mobius strip. This little device was discovered by August Ferdinand Mobius, a German mathematician, in 1858. Its properties never cease to amaze students.

MAKING THE STRIP

Take a strip of paper fourteen inches long by two inches wide. Give the strip of paper a half-twist just before pasting the ends together. Use cellophane tape to hold it together. The result is a completed mobius strip.

USING THE STRIP

1. If you draw a continuous line along the surface of the mobius strip, it is possible to go over the entire surface without ever crossing the edge. If you paint one surface of the band, there will be nothing left to paint. As a result, the mobius strip is often called a one-sided figure.

2. If you cut the mobius band lengthwise along a line through the center of the band, you obtain a somewhat surprising result. Rather than two mobius bands, you will obtain one large band, but with the "normal" two surfaces. If you now cut this figure along a line drawn lengthwise down its center, you will obtain two two-surfaced bands, linked within each other, impossible to separate.

3. If you cut the original mobius band lengthwise along a line that is about one third of the way across its surface, you will make two trips across the band, but only one cut. The result of this cut will be two strips intertwined; one will be a new mobius band, the other a two-surfaced figure.

CHANCE — A NORMAL CURVE

Students are often unaware of the many places wherein a so-called "normal" curve occurs. This random choice, bell-shaped curve has been discussed in many classes. Here is one way for the pupils to obtain a picture of this curve.

MAKING THE AID

Rule a piece of paper into one inch columns. Place a large dot in the center of the paper. Use the boxes at the bottom for tallying purposes.

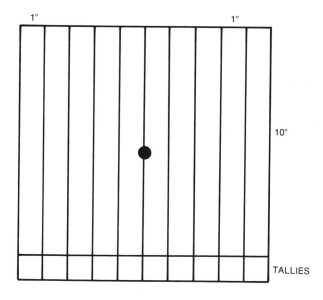

Figure 68.

USING THE AID

Count out exactly one hundred grains of uncooked rice into each of several envelopes. Have a pupil place the ruled paper on his desk and stand over it. The student should drop a few grains of rice at a time over the dot or center of the paper. When he has dropped one hundred grains, have another pupil in his group tally the number of grains of rice that have landed in each section. Count a line as belonging to the section wherein more of the rice lies.

The paper should now be cleared, the rice recounted, and the experiment repeated by other students. The height should be varied each time.

Have the class results drawn on a graph. Each group can draw a graph of its own results, but the class totals should provide a more accurate curve. Graph the number of grains against the columns, as shown in the figure. The result should be an S-shaped or bell-shaped curve.

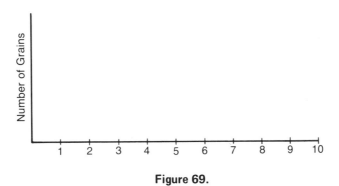

Figure 69.

PROBABILITY BOARD

When work in statistics and probability is introduced in the classroom, terms such as frequency, distribution, normal distribution, bell curve, probability, and so on, are discussed, often in the abstract. The probability board is a device that can be used to discuss these terms from a more concrete point of view. It should be used together with the normal curve device described in Aid Forty.

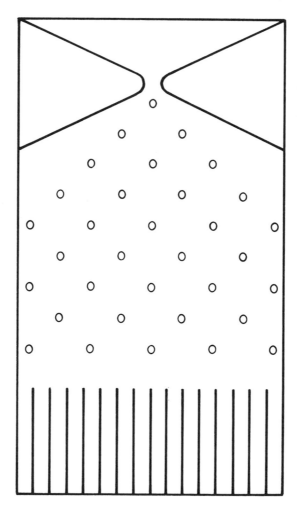

Figure 70. Probability board.

MAKING THE BOARD

A board of one-quarter inch plywood or pine is used as a base. It should be about eighteen inches long by twelve inches wide. Sides of one-eighth inch thick plywood are nailed all around the baseboard. These sides should be about three inches high. A number of brads are driven into the baseboard in rows of increasing numbers. Thus, the first row will have one brad, the second row will have two, the third three, and so on. The number of rows is optional. Cover about one-third of the board, beginning about one-third of the way down. At the top of the board, place a funnel type of barrier. Arrange this so that the first nail is directly underneath the opening. At the bottom, directly under the last row of nails, place a series of dividers, made of either thin plywood or heavy cardboard. Cover the entire device with a piece of plastic or heavy plastic wrap.

USING THE BOARD

Hold the board in an upright position. This is best done by leaning the bottom on a desk or a table or a pile of books. Have a student pour an envelope full of small metal balls or BB shot into the funnel at the top. As the balls fall toward the bottom, they will hit the nails and bounce off in either direction. They should work their way to the bottom, filling the slots with a bell-shaped or normal curve.

After doing this several times, it is possible to demonstrate skewness of a curve by slightly tipping the board to the right or left. Again, the balls will fall into a normal pattern, but will be skewed to either the left or the right.

The balls can be poured back into the top through the funnel by turning the entire board upside down and shaking it. It is also possible to make the bottom side of the board removable, and allow the balls to fall out this way.

INDEX

Note: Those entries in **boldface** are aids, games, or puzzles.